BUSINESS LEADERSHIP AND COMMUNITY

PERSPECTIVES ON DEVELOPING YOUR BUSINESS COMMUNITY

#1 BESTSELLER

JASON MILLER

FOREWORD BY JAMES DONALDSON

CHRIS O'BYRNE, WILL BLACK, AMY BLAIN, JAMES FOO TORRES, TERRY FOSTER, MIKE JACKSON, ALEXIA KAZ, MELANIE KOSSAN, SHELBY JO LONG, OTIS MCGREGOR, MIKE OWENS, JOEL PHILLIPS, MICHAEL SIPE, MIKE STEWARD

ISBN: 978-1-64184-838-1 (hardback)

ISBN: 978-1-64184-837-4 (paperback)

ISBN: 978-1-64184-836-7 (ebook)

Table of Contents

FOREWORD

JAMES DONALDSON, NBA ALL-STAR

FOUNDER OF YOUR GIFT OF LIFE FOUNDATION

I am proud to write this foreword for Jason Miller and team's newest book, *Business Leadership and Community*. I have known Jason for several years and have always been impressed by his business acumen and willingness to lend a helping hand whenever needed. This new book on community adds multiple perspectives on community from the viewpoint of business leaders.

Why is community important from a business perspective? One reason is that businesses do not thrive in a vacuum. Businesses need to form their own communities, and they also need to be active participants in other communities.

Another reason is that business leaders often have unique and powerful perspectives to contribute to any community they join. Just as we benefit greatly from the communities of which we're members, we also feel driven to help others benefit from our experience and skills.

Community adds to the rich fabric that makes up our society. We are all part of a "village," and we need each other to be successful and to move ahead.

Over the years, my communities have helped me because they have allowed me to serve in the community and to serve the people. I've been able to get involved within the education sector, business and commerce sectors, and the political sector. If you're willing to give first, with integrity, you will be rewarded many times over.

I have helped my communities, especially with my businesses, by heavily investing into them. I would always hire from the community first, and also provided internships and mentorships for the young people of the community.

When I get involved with a community, I get involved with the educational aspect, such as being a mentor to the young students, speaking at school assemblies, and being a positive male role model. I also get involved with the various Chambers of Commerce and civic groups such as Rotary and Kiwanis. These are all excellent ways to get involved with the community and to help out where you can.

Although online communities can be very powerful, I prefer community gatherings that are local and person-to-person. We need that human touch, and we only get that from congregating together. Online communities serve a purpose, but they are too impersonal for me.

My advice is to get involved with your community in as many different areas as you can. Volunteering is a wonderful way to get involved and to meet the people of the community. Mentoring our young people is another excellent way to give back. Being a positive role model for our youth is very much needed now, and we all could reach out and help.

Enjoy the many perspectives on business leadership and community presented in this book. And then take action. Join a community that would benefit from your expertise and perspectives. Form a new community and invite as many people into it as you can. Your business—and the world—will thank you.

James Donaldson

Your Gift of Life Foundation
yourgiftoflife.org

INTRODUCTION

CHRIS O'BYRNE

The topic of this bestselling book is timely and overdue. Community and business leadership go hand-in-hand, and no business lasts long without either one. A successful business, even a business of one, relies on and is enhanced by a strong and supportive community. And communities are only as supportive as the leaders within that community.

This book shares the perspectives on community of several successful business leaders. Jason Miller is the leader who brings all of us other leaders together in one strong community. All the authors are either directors of the Strategic Advisor Board (SAB) or are strategic partners of SAB. Jason is the founder and CEO of SAB and has gathered ten directors and a couple of hundred strategic partners, all of them powerful leaders and superb humans.

James Donaldson wrote the foreword and is a long-time friend of Jason Miller's. He's also a former NBA All-Star, playing with such powerhouse teams as the SuperSonics, the Clippers, the Mavericks, the Knicks, the Jazz, and the Harlem Globetrotters. He is the founder of the Your Gift of Life Foundation and the Donaldson Clinic. We're honored to include his foreword.

Will Black is a SAB director and CEO of Sharing the Credit. His chapter shows how you can support charity *and* save money by using the right credit card processing company. But there's much more to it than that, and Will shows us how to beat our competition through our program of giving.

Amy Blain is the founder of ExplorePeoria.com, a local events and entertainment directory. She has spent years learning how to support and improve her local community by leveraging her strong marketing background. Her perspective on building a local community is insightful.

James Foo Torres is the founder and CEO of Imperium Authority, a public relations firm. "Foo" has provided amazing PR services for all the SAB directors and earned his position on the cover of the premier issue of PIVOT Magazine. He shows us how media can both create and build community.

Terry Foster is the founder and CEO of Terry Foster Consulting, a premier digital marketing agency focusing on social selling. He has managed over $20 million in ad spend, leveraging it to over $75 million in sales for his fortunate clients. He takes us through his entire system, demonstrating the importance of community in his business.

Mike Jackson is a SAB director and the CEO of SF Consulting, which focuses on the medical industry. Mike was in the US Army with Jason Miller and has a strong background in Special Operations. Mike has some amazing stories and a powerful perspective on community.

Alexia Kaz is a rising star. She started selling on eBay when she was nine years old and started her own successful, full-service digital marketing agency before she was twenty. She has a deep perspective on the value of community, and despite her young age, she has the wisdom of someone much older.

Melanie Kossan is the founder and CEO of Mountain Mama LLC. She started out with a small cottage business selling hemp products and then discovered the life-changing power of CBD. From there, she has built a successful business and started both a national association and her own magazine. Melanie's business is both online and local, and her experiences with her local community, combined with her online communities, are enlightening.

Shelby Jo Long is a SAB director and the founder and CEO of Business Dynamics. She is also the CEO of Rogue Publishing Partners and a college professor. Shelby is a brand expert and teaches us a lot about community. I especially appreciate what she teaches about mastermind communities.

Otis McGregor is a retired US Army Lieutenant Colonel. Otis was one of the elite commanders of the Green Berets and provides a great military perspective on community. However, Otis has formed his own popular community called Tribe and Purpose. Read this chapter to learn about this unique community.

Mike Owens is a SAB director and the founder and CEO of MACO Consulting. Mike has been in the food and restaurant business most of his life, owning grocery stores and restaurants. He discovered his true calling, however, when he discovered how much he loved serving his business community.

Joel Phillips, another SAB director, is also the founder and CEO of ProShark, a full-service digital marketing agency. Joel shows us how important it is to have our own community platform. He feels so strongly about this that he has developed mPro, the ultimate community platform.

Mike Steward is the founder and CEO of Vision Fox Business Advisors, which provides business brokering, business coaching, and franchise services. Mike shares the two main roles of communities and how to get even more out of your communities.

I hope you both enjoy learning the perspectives these business leaders share about community.

To learn how you can become an author in our next international bestseller, please email me at chris@jetlaunch.net.

Chris O'Byrne

Founder and CEO of JETLAUNCH Publishing
Director and VP of Publishing for the Strategic Advisor Board
Director and VP of Publishing for Rogue Publishing Partners

Rich Communities Are Not Wealthy Communities

Jason Miller

Community is one of the most important aspects of starting and growing a business and can be very powerful. Your communities are where you can provide value and help others. Unfortunately, most people and businesses are all about taking. They join a community looking for how they can get paid. That's called the "rich" way of thinking because you are only focused on money. Rich thinking is about taking, not giving.

"Wealthy" thinking, on the other hand, is about so much more. It's about giving, not taking. Wealth includes so much more than money. It includes love, compassion, helping people, and more. It's about all those things they say are most important to people on their deathbed. When we build a community, then we automatically build wealth. The community as a whole gets to capitalize on that.

A good example of this is the strategic partner group for the Strategic Advisor Board. It is a community of like-minded people that gives back to each other and supports the whole organization. Building a community builds an ecosystem where everyone has the desire and ability to help each other.

The money will come, but you have to focus on creating a tight-knit community. That creates wealth.

I have also chosen to become part of communities that are all about giving back, and that is their main mission. I'm a part of a group called the Bellwether Alliance, for example, and giving back is what they're all about.

There are multiple rings or levels of community. Somebody once told me that a community doesn't have to be hundreds of people. In fact, one of the best communities is the ten people you are closest to. You know those people will always be there for you. When you go through hardship, when you're in need, then you find out who your real friends are.

The next ring is your good friends. Maybe you don't barbecue together on the weekend, but you are good friends. You get together to talk now and then.

Then there's the next ring, your acquaintances. These are people you talk to once every few months, but you know you could call them if you needed to, say, borrow their truck to move a big piece of furniture.

The last ring includes all those people you interact with about once a year or longer. And all of these rings form your circle of influence.

Communities are designed to be leveraged; that's why they exist. If we leverage communities right, we create an ecosystem of wealth. Wealth, not money, is what we should all be striving for.

People sometimes ask me how they go about figuring out what to give, but I think that's a basic human skill. I've also heard people say, "Go be your most authentic self." Since when was that so hard? Are we trying to be somebody else? It's the same concept when it comes to community. Just be yourself and find people who are like you. If you act like someone you are not, then you'll find people who are not like you.

There are many communities I would not fit in at all. I wouldn't join Mary Kay because it's not my circle of influence. It's about finding people who are like you and then culturing those relationships to build your community.

And this depends on what kind of community you're trying to create. You might be trying to create a business community, which is what this book is about, but there's also the personal community that feeds into the business community. I think they all kind of go hand in hand. We have this our personal circle, then the next circle, then the next, and so on.

In business, creating that really good balance of community relationships with other business owners creates referral pipelines. It creates friendship pipelines. It creates all these different pipelines. I know that sounds mechanical, but at the end of the day, that's what it is.

In business, we want to sell a product or service. At a surface level, that's why we develop business relationships: to sell our product or service. But we can approach community and relationships in a much more holistic way that's about nurturing versus "give me your money." Provide value to a community, and the community will give back. To find or build these nurturing communities, simply find like-minded people and start giving back. Just get involved.

I think every situation dictates how to build relationships. The way I build a relationship with one neighbor will look a little different from how I build a relationship with my other neighbor because one neighbor is eighty and the other is thirty-nine. Relationships are customized for each person or group of people. Our relationships at an annual event are different from at our parents' house. It's a natural human reaction to morph in a situation and still be your authentic self.

How do you make a relationship? Well, how did you meet your spouse? Did you just walk up to them the first time you met and say, "Hey baby, you're awesome. Let's go get married." That's not how it worked. You had to invest time and have a lot of conversations. It's the same thing with any relationship; it's just a different setting. If you really want to culture a relationship, including business relationships, it's not a one-and-done deal. You have to make time to get to know each other.

I went out for coffee with somebody recently, and we chatted for about an hour. It was really good to have that face-to-face contact, and we were really able to connect because of that conversation. Do we fully trust each other yet? No, but that will come with further conversations. You have to get away from the devices and actually talk to people. Get out there and actually make yourself a part of the community, make yourself known, give, have conversations, and the rest will fall in place itself.

If you want to start your own community, my best advice is not to wait, just start doing it. Start making connections with people who are like-minded and start having conversations. Go have a coffee. Have a beer. Smoke a cigar. Have a scotch. Whatever it is that you do, start building a relationship. Make a conscious effort to build a relationship. That's the secret right there. Put the devices down, stop texting, and start talking. I probably have upwards of ten to fifteen new conversations every week because I want to know more people. I am expanding my sphere of influence. I am expanding my reach. Just get out there and talk to people.

Over the years, I have started many communities of my own. The other nine directors of the Strategic Advisor Board are my closest inner circle of business relationships, followed closely by our strategic partners. Our strategic partner community

BUSINESS LEADERSHIP AND COMMUNITY

consists of about 200 strategic partners who span the gamut of pretty much every niche you could ever imagine. It's a great community of people, and it takes work to stay engaged and to keep giving value. I want everyone in that group to feel they're valued and heard, which takes a lot of work in a community that size.

In summary, I think we should all make a big effort to have conversations again. Over the last few years, we have become more disconnected than ever before. Let's build or rebuild our rings or levels of community and relationships. Let's build our local communities again. Let's support other local businesses and charities. It doesn't mean we have to throw away our non-local connections, but local connections fill a deep-seated need in all of us. And the work we do locally expands outward until our reach becomes global.

Go be authentic, be yourself, dream it, believe it, and then achieve it.

About Jason Miller

Jason is a seasoned CEO with an overwhelming passion to help other business owners and CEOs succeed. He is nicknamed Jason "The Bull" Miller because he takes no BS and no excuses from the people he serves. He has mentored thousands of people for over twenty years. Jason's major strengths are in project management, hyper company growth, scaling, strategic, and operational implementation. Jason has built several companies of his own from the ground up since 2001.

Jason has a specialty in helping businesses create a passive system of income and guiding other business owners through the rough waters of growing and scaling their company in sequence.

Jason currently operates The Strategic Advisor Board, Miller & Company, as well as other companies with multiple brands, which includes a full-service marketing agency, a staffing agency, and a government contracting branch where services can be provided for multiple agencies of the US Government.

Jason is a bestselling published author in the business world, including a 3x international bestseller. His seven published books have been featured at Barnes and Noble, stores world-wide, and Amazon. Jason donates all his book sales to "Homes for Heroes," of which donations have played a part in building multiple homes for Wounded Warriors. Jason has also been featured in Voyage Denver Magazine twice for being one of Colorado's most inspiring companies. He has also been fea-tured on Forbes, Entrepreneur, ABC, FOX, NBC, CBS and many more. Jason holds an MBA in business and continues to educate himself as a life-long learner.

Jason is also the creator of the famous Strategic Advisor Board podcast "War Room Round Table" (top 1.5% podcasts world-wide) where him and his co-host, the prior podcast host of Entrepreneur and Inc. Magazine's podcast, talk about business and how we leave a footprint.

Jason and his wife also spent a combined 25 years in the service to their country in the United States Army, while simultaneously growing and scaling multiple businesses and setting them on auto-pilot with the correct staffing and sys-tems put in place.

If you need help with hyper-growth and scaling your company in the proper sequence, that's where Jason can assist your company to the next level.

Learn more about Jason Miller at strategicadvisorboard.com.

Your Competition Wins If They Support a Charity

WILL BLACK

A whopping 80% of buyers will jump from their brand loyalty to another product *if* that product meets one and only one criterion. Right now, you're thinking that you know what it is. It's the money factor, right? The second one is cheaper. You would be wrong.

The second brands *gives*. It has a charity or a cause associated with it. As a matter of fact, not only will the customer jump from their normal product that they like and is a known commodity in their lives to the charity-endorsed product, but they will jump even if the second one is more expensive (as long as it isn't prohibitively more expensive).

The Cone Communications Report that studied this still had more to teach, however. The 80% rule seems to be a feel-good status that the donating product gives an emotional double-coupon day. You needed the macaroni/ shampoo/ olive oil anyway, so you might as well buy the one that also does some good. The funny thing was that it didn't have to be the buyer's cause. It was simply *a cause*. You might give to the United Way, but the spaghetti gives water to puppies in Iraq. Who doesn't like puppies? Your family always participates in an Alzheimer's fundraiser, but this frozen pizza donates to homeless vets. We like to feel like we are making good and healthy choices, and so we brand jump to the one that is doing the work to make the world a slightly better place.

The 80% doesn't apply to everyone, though. If you are a mom or a millennial, it's 90%. Right now, you should be rethinking your entire business plan. Mom's do the vast majority of the shopping for entire households (a thankless job, according to my wife, who just so happens to be a mom and the shopper for our home). As well, Millennials are known to be the primary purchasers and they will pay more for the items they like and that's not just kale chips and beard oil. Align this with your product and you have a sub-nuclear explosion of good vibes. You are an Alpo family when it comes to dog food. Your mom bought Alpo. Your grandparents bought Alpo. Obviously, God endorses Alpo in your mind, right? You go to buy Alpo for your beloved pooch, and you see between the Alpo and Gravy Train a big bag of Kibbles 'n Bits. Now you are not a Kibbles family, but there on the bag it says, "Buy this bag of Kibbles 'n Bits brand dog food, and we'll donate a bag of Kibbles 'n Bits dog food to a local no-kill dog shelter."

You're done.

Seriously. You are a dog person because you are buying dog food. The donation that *costs you nothing* gives to dogs. That is a perfect storm for creating a reason for customers to flock away from you to the competition. Tom's Shoes is either incredibly servant-minded or incredibly mercenary. He built in giving into the entire business model. Buy a pair of shoes and a pair is donated. Tom's is doing very well. I know people that have donated five pairs of shoes per family member, because they buy all their shoes from Tom's.

In the back of your mind, you know this. It's why we've seen shifts in the corporate world speaking more and more openly about their giving. You've seen it on cereal boxes, commercials. I even got a flyer at an Arby's drive-thru (don't judge me), about their support of feeding children who don't get a lot to eat. Earlier you thought you knew the answer, and that it was money. You were right. It's just that people like that their money is doing some good.

There is one important caveat to mention here and now. Transparency. We have grown up seeing ads our entire life. We've seen too many examples of a company donating $500,000 and then spending $2,000,000 advertising the gift. This poisons the well. Consumers are extraordinarily savvy in these fields, and they like to see the giving. Not to mention there are always watchdogs looking for something that doesn't smell right. Give. Give cleanly. Give transparently. People want to give. It's like it's in our DNA. That many people in the Cone Communications study simply can't be that off. We want to give. We WANT it. Why do you think the Salvation Army is out front of all the department stores come Christmas? It's not because of little Ralphie trying to get a Red Ryder BB gun. It's because they know we want to give. Unlike Santa Claus, this is the gift that can give all year long.

A second caveat would be that you have to make it easy. Our Alpo-buying friend moved to Kibbles because all he had to do was grab the bag and pay for it like anything else. He came to the store to do just that. However, if he bought Alpo and the cashier pestered him with, "Do you want to add a dollar? Do you want to round up? Do you want to buy this paper heart and put your name on it for $1 to show that you love dogs?", he might go for it, but he won't feel as good. In fact, he'll hate it and even start avoiding the store outright if they do it more than once or twice a year. I stopped going to one store as for 6 months they never missed a beat in asking me for more money as a donation. 6 months. That is not on my terms. That is now putting me on the spot and making me feel bad if I don't give. Just give me the milk, please. Don't sour it.

Easy giving, in this case, makes easy customers and happy thoughts. My company, Sharing the Credit, builds in automatic philanthropy into each and every business we deal with. In the modern world, everyone pays in plastic. Debit card or credit card doesn't matter, but if your company doesn't have a merchant account that lets people pay you in plastic; you're out of business. Well, every time a customer comes into your store and swipes a card, or goes online and enters their card data, one of the fees that Visa/MC takes out doesn't go to Visa/MC. It goes back into the system, and normal to a bank; but it can go to a charity. Not my charity, but your charity. Think about it. Your business has no choice but to pay Visa/MC at the end of the month. Would you rather a portion go to put a bank president in a new Lexus, or save those puppies in the no-kill shelter? Me? I'm a dog person.

What's your company supporting? And are you letting people know?

About Will Black

Will is steeped in the world of merchant accounts and knows the ins and outs of how businesses suffer headache and financial damage via their companies most needful operation: Getting paid in plastic. He has spent three decades in the industry working with hospitals, the military, and everything from the smallest of start-ups to multimillion-dollar-a-month operations. He regularly cuts through the tape and jargon and shows other CEO's and college business classes how they get over-charged, and how to avoid it.

Will specializes in showing non-profits how they can get massive funding from the businesses that support them already by the redirection of a built-in fee that creates long term, sustainable funding. He has given away $1,000,000+ and is on the $10,000,000 mission now, and most impressively: all in unrestricted funds.

Will started and runs Sharing the Credit and which works with non-profits and their donor companies, and regularly trains non-profits and their development staff in the secret knowledge of merchant accounts.

Will sits on a number of boards including the Coastal Jail Ministry, his local Rotary, Thrivent, and as a member of the Diaconate of his church. He wrote the book Paid in Plastic: The Art of the Steal, which trains business owners how to do a month's worth of math in 30 seconds. One professor said it should be used as a business primer in college classes for anyone who thought to own a business. He is an Amazon bestselling author, an international bestselling author and has written for several business periodicals and been published in TheArtofManliness.com.

Learn more about Will Black at sharingthecredit.com.

Local Community and Business

Amy Blain

M y background is in television and advertising, and I worked in those fields for twenty-five years. I began at my local NBC affiliate TV station doing promotions, a lot of which were advertising to promote the TV station overall and the news programs specifically. I then moved to our local civic center as the marketing manager.

Because of my work at the civic center and my involvement as a teenager in my local community theatres, I had quite a bit of experience with local entertainment and events happening in my area.

At some point, while I was working at the civic center, it became clear to me that the only way to really make any money was by going into sales. I made the transition, which was terrifying because I went to a relatively small base salary plus commission, so there was no real guarantee of my income. At the time, my husband had begun his video production company, so neither of us would have a guaranteed salary other than my small base.

However, I'm glad I did it because I essentially became an entrepreneur even though I was employed with a salary and benefits. I sold for two different TV stations, then I sold for the billboard company for five years, and then I also did a brief stint selling ads for Cars.com.

After working for several companies and dealing with them reducing my commissions, plus their ability to take away clients on their whim, I began to think, *Why am I breaking my back selling ads for these media companies? I should be building my own media property and have something to show for all my years of hard work.*

Meanwhile, the internet happened, and I was fascinated by it. I knew it was going to change the way people did everything, especially shopping and marketing products, services, and events. I wanted to be a part of that because it sounded interesting and challenging. I knew it was going to be the way of the future, and that way I could maybe build my own media empire and profit from that as opposed to working for some company that didn't really care about their clients.

When I work with my clients, since I own the company, I can do whatever I want. I can be flexible and work with them, and they really appreciate that. I don't have to appease any corporate overlords as other sales reps do.

Going off on my own represented freedom for me and the opportunity to do what I am passionate about. Since my background was in events and entertainment, I chose to pursue building a website that helped people find out what was going on in the area. Before that, there was an organization of five different nonprofit organizations in the area, like the chamber of commerce, the convention bureau, the realtor association, and a couple of others that built a huge website. They spent what they thought was a lot of money. My former intern from my civic center days, who was the marketing person at the convention bureau at the time, kept me abreast of what was going on with that.

I thought if they were investing money in this, there must be something to it. It used to be that if you subscribed to the newspaper, you would know what was going on in the area. But with the decline of the newspaper industry, people were left hanging and had no idea how to find the information unless they went to each of the venue websites individually. I realized I could package all of that on one website so that it was more convenient.

I started in 2007, which I like to joke is like "dog years" in internet time. So much has changed since then. A lot of sites similar to mine have come and gone. The main one fell apart around the time I began, and recently, our convention bureau began using that old domain name again for their website.

The convention bureau targets people from outside the community and tries to bring them into the city but still tries to reach residents too, which is my target audience. They receive a lot of funding from the state and the federal government, while I'm just a little entrepreneur doing my own thing. So, we approach it from different angles.

I started my website, Explore Peoria, because I love helping people figure out what's going on locally. This type of site run by a local entrepreneur is kind of unique. I recently spoke to a promoter about a month ago who brought in a Monster Truck Wars event to my area, and he said, "This is great. I love working with you." I said, "Don't you wish you had someone like me in all the markets you go to?" He said, "I do; it would be so much easier." It's hard to buy media to promote events, especially for organizations that are just coming into a market only once or twice a year.

I work with people like that who are from outside the market, but I also work with a lot of local organizations that are mostly nonprofits, like the community theaters and a lot of other performing arts organizations. I work with some of the festivals, too. Today, we were just shooting a video for the Heart of Illinois Fair to help them promote that. We do probably five or six different festivals throughout the year.

One of my biggest clients is the local museum. We work with a lot of different entities, and the way we monetize the site is through more traditional advertising. Luckily, my husband owns a video production company, and he's been on his own for just under thirty years. I roped him into helping me do what we call entertainment report videos.

He has also been involved in the local theater organizations, helping them with sound and other technical things. This has allowed us to do things that no one else is really doing. The convention bureau used to do some videos with their spokesperson a few years ago, but they don't do videos as we do. I used to get their newsletter twice a month, but I haven't even gotten it lately. I have a feeling it's probably in my spam folder. They would only highlight a couple of organizations, so it never had nearly as much content as my newsletter.

I can offer my advertisers the standard banner ad type of thing on the website, and I also do articles. I just did one about staycations in the area. With gas prices so high, it's so expensive to drive and fly right now, plus it's just a headache. People want to get out and do things now that COVID is starting to move into the rearview mirror. I wrote the article highlighting a dozen or so events, like the Heart of Illinois Fair or the museum's latest exhibit. I also included several other park district attractions as well as concerts down on the Peoria riverfront. Along with that, I am running a contest where

I'm giving away passes or tickets to those various attractions and events.

One of the other big elements of the business, and it's probably the thing that has brought in the most revenue overall, was building my email list. I started a newsletter shortly after I started the website. All the internet marketers say the money is in the list, and that's definitely the case.

I'm doing it a little differently than they do because I'm doing it on a local level. I'm not asking those individual people who are on my list to buy things from me. It's monetized a little differently than a traditional email list. Because of my background working at the civic center, I knew that contests were a very effective way to get the word out about events. So, I started doing contests, and once people signed up for the contest, they were automatically subscribed to my newsletter, which is free. That's really what has built my email list over the years, and I continue to run contests today.

I used to put every single event that was on my calendar in my email newsletter, and that could be close to forty events every week. That was a lot, especially as people moved to reading their email on their smartphones with a much smaller screen, so I decided I needed to update the way I handled my newsletter. I had been thinking about doing this for years after I watched what Mike Cooch was doing in San Diego.

When COVID happened, and I wasn't sending out the newsletter because nothing was going on, I realized that when I started sending it out again was the perfect time to make the transition. I didn't want to do it abruptly. Now I do newsletter sponsorships vs. display ads (they were skyscraper ads and were super narrow and difficult to see on a mobile phone). Everybody who is included in my newsletter now is either a paid or trade ad. It's not really an ad; it's actually content marketing. I only include between five and eight events now as opposed to the forty or so I included before. I have a nice big picture of each event, then a line or two of text, and a link to their website or Facebook event page. It's much cleaner and more interesting for my subscribers.

Before the pandemic hit, I had a little over 21,000 subscribers, which for the Peoria market is a pretty nice number. We're at about 100,000 metro population. So that's about a fifth of the population in this area. I was a little nervous when I started to send the newsletter out again after taking that year and a half off. I had been doing it for fifteen years, and there were a lot of people who had been on my list for a long time. When I started it up again, I was gratified to see that the people kept opening it and clicking and were still looking for that information, probably even more so because they wanted to get out and do things now that they finally could.

I send the newsletter out every Thursday afternoon, and that's become the main way that I get the information out to people, even more so than the website. People also go to the website, and one of the main features is our big event calendar. So, they'll go and check that out. There are also a lot of people who just get the newsletter, and they'll click on the link to the event calendar to find out what is happening in the area.

The idea with the updated newsletter format is to get people interested in the event so that they want to get more information and click to go to the website or their Facebook page to get all the nitty gritty. I also have a link to my events calendar at the bottom of every newsletter, plus I include links to my current feature articles. It's a lot more user-friendly, especially when viewed on a phone. I think that has made the newsletter even more attractive than it used to be.

Also, the advertisers like it because it's not ads. They're just part of it; it's just a picture with a link and a bit of text. So, it doesn't appear to the reader as paid advertising—it's just news. It's evolved a little over the years.

I was on the board of two of the three community theaters a few years ago, so I knew that they didn't have a lot of money to get the word out about their shows, and they're constantly challenged. That's why we do a lot of the things we do. I feel their pain because I have been on the boards of organizations that needed help.

That's why we developed our entertainment reports. Those are all the videos that my husband does for me, and they're extremely popular. He calls it Mr. Rogers style because there's no reporter. The interviewees speak straight to the camera so that it feels like they're talking right to the viewer and makes it more personal. It's not like the news; it's more of an infomercial. I would consider it content marketing. I don't know if the organizations that I work with see it that way because they're not really marketers for the most part, but in essence, that's what it is.

We added the videos about four or five years ago. I had wanted to do an entertainment report video for a while, but it was something I felt needed to be consistent. That was difficult because my husband is so busy with his video production business, especially during basketball and hockey season when he's doing a lot of games for our civic center. But he's been very good about that, and I think it's a fun project for him.

We'll interview one of the directors of a show, if it's a theater show, and then maybe a cast member, too. We just did one for a local children's theatre. They're doing *Aladdin*, so we interviewed the actors playing Jafar, Aladdin, and Jasmine. We asked them to record a personal invitation for people to come to see the show and then talk about what it meant to them to be involved with the show.

For instance, the kids who played Jasmine and Aladdin said that they've been waiting to do this show together for years. They were really happy to be able to do that finally with this show. They always have great stories to tell about being in the cast with the other kids that they meet because it's a community show; it's not only kids from their school but kids from all over the community that they may not have met otherwise. It's fun to let them tell their story.

We then post that on our website, YouTube channel, and Facebook page. The community theater share's that on its Facebook page, and then the cast, crew, and parents can share it as well. This particular organization is really good about that, and we got around sixty shares within a day or two.

It's fun to be able to really help these organizations because that's my passion—to help them. It also helps the community to learn about that in a way that they wouldn't necessarily be able to do, just with an ad. And these organizations don't have much to spend on marketing. They typically only spend about $500 to market a show at most.

We keep it inexpensive, and we have a package that includes the video plus a banner ad, a newsletter sponsorship, and a solo ad that's very popular. Usually, my husband shoots the first act of one of the dress rehearsals when shooting for a theatrical production. For *Aladdin*, they have a fly system where the kids fly on the magic carpet on the stage. So, he's got video of the kids and their costumes on the set with the lighting and the special effects. People get a good idea of what the show is going to be like through these videos.

We hope the videos help sell tickets for them, which is the bottom line, but it's also fun to be able to show people in the community what this organization is doing.

Getting involved in your community depends on the market, but there are all kinds of organizations out there. If you're going to a brand-new community and are looking to meet people and find out what's happening and get involved, I think the best thing to do is to volunteer. There are all types of nonprofit organizations that are desperate for volunteers who want to be there and want to make a difference in their community.

There are a lot of different opportunities available. You could volunteer at a community theater doing props for a show. We have an organization called Neighborhood House, and they teach people in the community who are illiterate how to read. A lot of those things can be extremely rewarding and get you out to meet people you would never meet otherwise.

This helps those people who you're trying to help, but it also helps you. It is satisfying to know that you're making a difference in your community. It's going to be unique to each area, but there are all kinds of ways to help, and nowadays, there are online forums that can help you get connected.

My best advice for someone starting out in business or building a website like mine is don't do it for the money; do it for the passion. I didn't really know what I was doing at the beginning of it all. I just was kind of taking what I knew, which was media sales, and trying to do my own thing, which I did. At this point, it's probably about as successful as it can be.

A lot depends on the market you're in. I was running Explore Peoria for many years, and then I found a gentleman, Mike Cooch, who has a very similar business that he developed in his market, but it was the same concept. He's in San Diego, so he has a much larger local community.

He has lots more resources and funding for his website, including a staff that writes articles for him. I have a part-time assistant who helps me post events on my calendar, but other than that, it's just me. I'm making sales, I'm laying out ads, I'm sending emails, I'm going on shoots for videos, I'm posting videos, and I'm writing articles and doing search engine optimization for the website. I wear a lot of hats.

It's a little easier for him to make some money because he can hire writers, and he is in such a big market. He can pay to boost his posts on Instagram and Facebook. I do a little bit of that, but he does way more. He spends big bucks on that, but again, he can do that. The ROI is there because he can sell it for more.

I don't have as much interactivity on my site and social properties as others may have. I did that by design because I know it's going to require a lot of time to monitor all of that. From a business standpoint, social media can be a lot to deal with. I can't believe some of the comments I have seen on some of the Facebook posts I've shared about our community. There's a lot of negativity in the world right now, and it's draining to deal with that. I'm in the business of good news, and I like to keep it positive.

One of the things I do with my email list is I allow the local event promoters like our museum to send out what I call solo ads, which is an Internet marketing term, but it's essentially an email blast. I only let event promoters do this with my email list because I don't want to have car dealers trying to hawk their cars to someone on my list because it's not really "in voice" with what ExplorePeoria.com is about. It's very limited, and the people who are on my subscriber list know that the information in emails from me is all going to be related to events and entertainment.

When I first started Explore Peoria, I had never built a website or anything. I had done TV production, and I'm relatively technical, so I knew I'd figure it out eventually. But initially, it was a little overwhelming.

I used a company that builds city directory websites, so it had the basic structure I was looking for, but it also it allowed me to create my own content. They hosted the site and did tech support. So, if I broke something, I knew they'd be there to fix it. And they had to do that a couple of times, early on.

But as time passed, I got more interested in learning about building my own websites. I learned how to build sites on Joomla, which now has mostly gone by the wayside. Then I really got involved with WordPress, which is what my site is currently built on. It is what a large majority of websites are now built on.

I've become a lot more adept at the technical stuff. I have learned a lot through building my email list and sending emails, working on social media and video, YouTube, and working on other social media platforms. It constantly evolves as you go, and you must keep learning how to do all the stuff that needs to be done.

Making your business financially viable can be tricky. I had experience in media sales, and if I hadn't had that, I would never have been able to make this profitable. And honestly, even with that, it took me many years because you have to have something to sell.

It's definitely been a labor of love for me, and it's given me a reason to pursue my interest on the internet and all that has changed over those years since I started. Again, for those wanting to make a lot of money, this may not be the right format, but I know that the nonprofit organizations that I work with appreciate what I've been able to do for them. It's nice to be able to help those organizations and make a difference for them in my local community.

About Amy Blain

Amy has been a seasoned advertising and strategy veteran for over thirty years. She studied mass communication at Illinois State University. She started working at the local NBC affiliate as an intern while in college and later worked there full-time after graduation.

She worked as the marketing manager at the Peoria Civic Center and later was an advertising specialist selling advertising for the Fox affiliate in her market. Amy then worked as an account executive for Adams Outdoor in Peoria as well as was the regional sales manager for the ABC and WB affiliates in her market. She was also a marketing specialist for Cars.com.

Most recently, Amy has owned a local online events and entertainment directory, ExplorePeoria.com, for her hometown for fifteen years. Because of her experience promoting her website over the years, she began helping other local businesses use the power of the internet to help grow their businesses. She published her book, *Local Digital Marketing Secrets*, in 2017, which is available for purchase on Amazon.com.

A wife and mom of one daughter and lifelong resident of Peoria, Illinois, she's lived in the historical district of Peoria for over thirty years. She has a passion for her local community and neighborhood.

Learn more about Amy Blain at ExplorePeoria.com.

The Importance of Community and Public Relations for Business Success

James Foo Torres

Media is communicating to the masses. In the past, media was mostly newspapers, TV, and radio, but now, it's all online and there are millions of websites and countless podcasts and digital magazines. Podcasts have become the new radio and online magazines typically have more authority and visibility than newspapers. Many of these Internet-based news outlets have better audiences and communities than radio and newspapers because of branding, social media, and effective marketing.

You can reach the entire world through the Internet, which is why the media is much more robust than ever before. You can even go live on your own platform, something that was difficult or nearly impossible even ten years ago. If you have a large following, you can get thousands of people to tune into your platform live.

Media can be anywhere where there are masses of people paying attention to a specific topic. It includes social media, podcasts, and online print magazines, and TV and radio are still a part of that. Furthermore, I would say that the U.S. media is one big audience ready to look at you and what you're doing.

Media also allows us to create community. Among the communities I value most is the Strategic Partners community from the Strategic Advisor Board (SAB). Even though I didn't create this community, it's one I feel deeply passionate about and like to contribute to. I have been a guest podcaster for the SAB podcast, where my segment is called *Moments with Foo*. I am also the CEO of Imperium Authority, the PR firm in charge of SAB's public relations. Additionally, I am very close to the board, especially with Jason Miller, the CEO.

Before being involved in business and business communities, back when I was in college, I wanted to belong to a fraternity or a similar community. I've always been a social person, but I didn't like the hazing and nonsense that fraternities do, and since I didn't believe in those things, I wanted to create my own.

One day, I was hanging out with my friends and thinking about how the first part of my last name is Foo, which is Chinese. I was thinking, *What if I had imperial blood?* Then, I thought, *I'll create my own empire.* So, in college, I was able to create part of my community that became a part of my empire. We are still close after many years. We're like family, but a family that I created. That's the reason my company is called Imperium Authority.

Regarding specific PR-related communities, I am part of a community called Profitable PR Pros. It has over 3,000 people, and it has been extremely valuable for me and all members I have talked to. I have met some great people in that group. We share resources, and we are constantly engaging, asking questions, and answering questions. So that's another wonderful group that I didn't create but am an integral part of. I am grateful to be part of a community like that.

There are so many benefits of being a part of communities. It is great to be able to provide value for people. Additionally, communities are important for opportunities in the media. With media and PR, you not only have to have great content, but you also must be able to reach out to the right people the right way. However, the right way is different depending on the person.

You must be able to make personal connections. Media features are something that everyone wants; however, most people don't know how to get it or don't understand it. You must offer value for both sides. For the media to care, they need to have some sort of connection, and they need to feel like they are getting value. It won't work to approach it like, "Hey, please feature my client or feature me because I'm so great and I deserve it." That doesn't come across well. Always look for ways to provide quality content, and don't forget to lead with value. That's why communities are so helpful. Communities provide a centralized location that is based on people adding value to each other.

You always want to lead with value as much as possible. Then when you ask for something, people will reply because they see you being active, and they see you are always giving value. They know that if they help you, you will help them in return. They see that everybody's helping each other, and everybody's getting value from it. That's one of the most important things that I get from the community. Being involved in a community leads to so many positive connections and referrals. Instead of sending cold emails, communities provide you with direct connections.

Leading with value is also the basis for how we create engagement. That is the main thing to always keep in mind. Additionally, to create engagement with my online communities, I like to share what I'm learning during my journey as a PR agency owner.

I'm always looking for new connections and new strategies because a lot of our public relations success is found in our strategy. We must think about how we reach out to people, what their focus is at the moment, and how we can offer value to them. Continuing to grow and learn allows me to share new experiences and add more value to my communities.

Furthermore, this strategy has shown me where the opportunities are. This, combined with the knowledge and strategy, is an incredible value to offer. That is what I do to leverage connections, create a response, and add value. When you lead with value, people then feel more inclined to give value to you in any way they can.

If you are debating if you should consider starting a PR strategy, the big, important questions are, "Why wouldn't I work on my public relations?" and "What's stopping me?" Those are the questions that I would like you to ask yourself.

If the reason that you're not doing it is because you don't feel like you are ready for it, you don't feel like you have a story to tell, or you don't feel like you have anything that the media wants, those are limiting beliefs. And remember, everybody has a story. And if you are successful, you have already figured something out, right? Because that's the one thing you must do first—you must figure it out. You must figure out what your superpowers are. What's the one thing you want to commit to?

Branding is also important. But after you have your branding solid and established, and you have some success, you want to add fuel to your fire. Now, you're ready to share your story. If you don't believe that the media wants your story, that's a limiting belief. If you talk with someone in PR, like me, and we look at your whole story, we will always find newsworthy angles because everybody has a story.

Even what you consider only a small success is important to share. To get to that success, you probably tried many things, you probably had to overcome a lot of challenges, and that's your story. That's something a lot of people would like to know. And when people can relate to your story, that's when they can really get behind your product or service, especially if it's unique. However, even if you do something common, like taxes or business coaching, we can still find what makes you different. Your unique story is what's in your background, your branding, and your "why." Those are what you want to share through trusted media sources, and that's why PR is so important. As a business owner, sharing your story with authority is vital.

About James Foo Torres

James Foo Torres is the CEO of Imperium Authority, a public relations firm. Imperium Authority specializes in helping business leaders become thought leaders. Ultimately, when you're in business, and you're seen as a thought leader and authority in your space, that's when people don't think twice about working with you. If people already need your services, and they see you as a clear authority, they don't feel the need to look anywhere else because why look anywhere else when the best is already in front of them.

Imperium Authority helps people create that feeling with their prospects. That's the main thing that we specialize in doing. We do this by focusing on media relations and strategies to maximize the impact of getting features in trusted media sources.

Learn more about James Foo Torres at imperiumauthority.com.

The Importance of Community Through a Business Pivot

TERRY FOSTER

I'm the owner and founder of Terry Foster Consulting, a digital marketing agency that has helped numerous brands scale to seven figures with profitable paid traffic. That's the business model that allowed me to clear $4 million dollars in revenue.

But the iOS 14.5 update really took a toll on the success that ecommerce businesses had with paid traffic because the cost to acquire customers has gone up significantly. Since then, we haven't been able to deliver quite the same level of results for ecommerce clients that we have always been able to because of all these things working against us.

I realized that I had to make a pivot, and I had to make a pretty big pivot with who we serve.

My new offer is called Scale with Social Selling, and our new target market is service-based businesses that are looking to have more sales conversations with their perfect prospects. That can be agencies, coaches, consultants—pretty much anyone who needs sales calls booked to grow their business. Social selling is the process of selling and connecting via direct messaging, such as Facebook DMs, Instagram DMs, and LinkedIn Messenger. That's the process we use to get sales calls with our client's perfect prospects!

Our "unfair advantage" is proprietary software that allows us to work far more efficiently so we can go out and add a lot of people into your pipeline. We can pull people from Facebook posts, not only if the business makes a post and people comment on it, but where a competitor made a post and had people comment on it. It can also be from either an organic post or a paid post. We can also pull people who have liked any post on Facebook. We do the same thing with Instagram and LinkedIn.

Being able to go out and quickly source prospects with a click of a button and get them into our pipeline allows us to work a lot more efficiently. We have helped businesses generate over $100 million of sales online. And even though this isn't paid traffic, this still very much has a direct-response component. In addition, my team is excellent at copywriting, and we know the psychology of engaging with someone and nurturing them to get them to take the desired action we're looking for.

We also have a proprietary system to train your sales team. This is very tedious. It's not hard work, but it's tedious work that needs consistency. You need a well-trained team. We have that so that we can provide a done-for-you solution so you can be totally hands-off. We book sales calls, and we have a guarantee on the number of calls we give clients based on the package they select.

When you start working with us, the first thing we have you do is meet with our customer success manager. We work together to make sure we're prospecting people from the right places because you know where your ideal prospects are. We also make sure we fully understand what your sales funnel looks like, making sure we're driving people into it correctly: *Do they take sales calls? Is it better to get someone to submit an application? Do we want to get someone to sign up for a webinar masterclass?*

All of that is communicated in the initial call, and then we take that information and develop our assets. We determine where we will pull people from, and we create a conversational flow for your pipelines. You get to see and approve the types of messages we send out and how the flow works to get people to book a call or submit an application.

Our job is to connect our clients with their perfect prospects so that they can close more sales. We guarantee the right type of people will be sent to you. We then deliver on our promise, giving you a guaranteed number of calls. If you close at least ten percent of these prospects, we know you will make money. All you have to do is make sure you can close and then properly fulfill those sales. The longer those clients stay with you, the more profitable your investment in us becomes.

Community is very important for us. One of our Facebook groups is called Paid Ads Mastery, and it is 2,600 people strong. That group allows us to show our expertise and provide social proof. We also run challenge launches where we draw people to the group, and then there is a theme or goal over the course of five days, like boosting sales or getting paid traffic. This helps wake up and engage the community.

Another community we have is our email list. We're very intentional about the type of emails we send, so they're not always sell, sell, sell. We establish a rapport and provide as much value as possible. As a result, our unsubscribe rate is very low.

We also have a paid community; a group coaching program called the Business Accelerator Group that helps business owners learn how to succeed with paid traffic. That's a paid community we pour into to make sure we maximize their stick rate with our program.

As we go through our pivot, our communities will also change, yet they will also stay the same in many ways. We will still have a free Facebook group and eventually do more challenges. We are growing this group with the exact process we're using with our clients. We lead by example, so once we grow the group via social selling, we'll accelerate that process by doing things such as challenges and upsell to our paid Facebook group.

The new Facebook group will be under the Terry Foster Consulting brand for now, but as it starts to pick up, I will splinter it off of the brand and create a new Facebook group because my existing community is mostly ecommerce brands. We have around 2,600 members in our Paid Ads Mastery group, but the majority of those people are ecommerce brands because that's what we are known for.

Our email list has around 5,500 people, and the majority of those are ecommerce brands. We can send some emails and pull out the people who aren't ecommerce, but we are mostly starting close to zero because the audience we're going after now is not the same audience we were going after before. We don't want it to be confusing.

Community building has been an integral part of building and scaling our business because people want to do business with people they know and trust. One way to do that is to create a community and then give them a lot of value. This should happen even before they give you any money. We also want our clients, customers, and students to share their experience working with our agencies, showing their screenshots of success and things like that. Once you can do that, and you have your current clients or customers inspiring other people, that's a big win for you. And that's a type of community as well because you get people to rally around you.

If you have a business, it's always in your best interest to have a community so you're visible and people know about you, which gives you the opportunity to demonstrate your expertise. When you have Facebook groups, for example, you want to make sure you're visible in there, that you're popping up and going live, saying hello, asking how people are doing, and developing relationships.

Relationships are very important, no matter what type of business you have. Relationships and community go hand in hand. You always want to leverage and create social proof. The perception of someone who has a big community and is engaged will be different from a business owner who has no community or a community where there's no engagement. You want to increase the perception of your brand.

Don't let building your community be an afterthought. Be intentional about it. The more intentional you are, the faster it will grow. A couple of ways to amplify your community are social selling and paid traffic. With social selling, you can reach out to people via DMs, tell them about your group, and try to get them to join that way.

There are a lot of ways you can quickly grow your community, but you also want quality over quantity. It's important to make sure that the people in your community get value from that community. If not, they'll leave. They must want to be there. Provide value and help them grow, even if you only help them discover something they didn't know before. In the long run, those are the people who will become your paying clients. Make sure you nurture that and treat your community like you would any other business relationship; it's that important.

Facebook groups are a good way to build a community. If you're more of a LinkedIn person, there are many LinkedIn groups as well. Think about what type of content you would be able to curate to provide value to that community. It doesn't mean you have to allocate forty hours a week to provide value to your community. It doesn't take that much time; just be intentional about how the time you spend. The more you can pour in, the more you'll get out of it. I would recommend that all business owners have some type of group they own.

Challenge launches definitely still work, although not as well as they used to. They are one of the best ways to quickly create a community because, if you're doing a group challenge launch, you will put some ad budget behind it. If it's hosted in your group, that will motivate those members.

Challenges are one of the best ways to combine quickly building a community while also monetizing that community. If someone spends five days with you on a challenge, and you give them quick wins and they see some growth, then, of course, some of those people want to take the next step, which is buying whatever you sell at the end of that challenge. Challenges definitely still work if you do them correctly.

I recommend you use different strategies and different channels to build your community. Some people only tap into paid traffic via Facebook ads, or maybe they only do social selling. You want to make sure that you diversify the ways you grow your community. That's something that not a lot of people do, but it can really help the growth of your community.

It's also important to realize that building your community is an investment. You can't always expect it to give you a return on investment on day one. As I said, some of those people may join your Facebook group today, and they may not buy and become a client until next year, and that's all right.

It's best you have the correct mindset that you're developing relationships and that some people will be ready to buy quickly while others will decide slowly. Make sure that you have the right expectations. If you go into it with the mindset of community first, and you actually want to pour into that community, people will feel that. You will make more money on the backend as opposed to only wanting the Facebook group because you only want to sell on it.

About Terry Foster

Terry Foster is the man behind helping hundreds of business owners fall back in love with their business by helping them scale their business via effective digital marketing strategies. Since 2016, Terry Foster Consulting has managed over $20 million dollars of ad spend, resulting in over $75 million dollars of sales. Terry is most proud of helping fourteen different businesses exceed $1 million dollars of sales in a calendar year.

Learn more about Terry Foster at terryfosterconsulting.com.

Helping Others Through Community
MIKE JACKSON

Jason Miller (the founder of Strategic Advisor Board) and I were infantrymen together a million years ago. It's been a while, but I remember. I had a midlife crisis, and I decided being an infantryman wasn't hard enough. So, I thought I should be a US Army Special Forces medic who also spoke Arabic.

I spent two years in training to become that. The course alone was fifty weeks long. It covered everything from clinical medicine to doing surgery and anesthesia, and I've used a lot of that overseas during my work. After getting qualified to do the work, I did that for twenty-seven years.

That opened a lot of doors and opportunities. My last active-duty job was teaching the two-week medical refresher that all Special Operations medics and all the services have to attend every two years. I taught that for about six years.

Halfway through that six-year period, I retired and became a contractor. I did a couple of different jobs at the Special Operations Medical School as a contractor. I did the regular medical refresher, and I helped build a surgical med refresher course.

Now I teach surgery and anesthesia full-time. Working in that Special Operations arena, I've had tons of wonderful opportunities to work with other service people. I work with a couple of Air Force retired aerospace medical doctors, and I teach jungle and dive medicine, usually in St. Croix, US Virgin Islands.

I also work with a local Boy Scout troop as their wilderness survival merit badge guy. Whenever they need a wilderness survival merit badge course run, I run that.

I am also an American Red Cross certified instructor, so I teach a wilderness and remote first aid course for Boy Scouts and Boy Scout leaders in the area. It's a fun sixteen-hour course and includes a lot about working in the woods. I get to use my experience from being a medic overseas to help guide my teaching, and it's a lot of fun.

I teach both in person and online. I help out with the Special Forces Medical Sergeant course on Fort Bragg at the Joint Special Operations Medical Training Center.

People ask me, "Have you ever had to do this overseas?" When they ask this, however, we're usually in a solid operating room with full sterile protocols. So I say, "The last time I did this overseas, I had a ballcap on, I was under a tarp outside, and had a cigar in my mouth. I had sterile gloves on, and that was about as sterile as I could be with the equipment I had. Sometimes you just got to pump them full of more antibiotics because you have nothing else to do for them."

I primarily worked in Iraq and spent multiple years there. There are five Special Forces groups, and each group has an area of responsibility in the world. Some work in Southeast Asia, some work in Europe, some work in Africa, some work in central South America—all over the world. The group I picked was the one that spoke Arabic in southwest Asia, so that's where I spent a lot of time.

I have been very lucky, because I've never had to do major work on any of my guys. I've never had any of my guys shot and had to fix him. I've been very, very lucky. Unfortunately, I've had to work on other fellow American service members.

I think every time I ever worked on an American service member, it was a roughest time because it was important. It didn't matter what was going on around me, if bullets were flying around over my head because I could turn all that stuff off. And all I did was focus on the patient. Those were rough times.

I relate more with the Special Forces medical community than the Special Forces community because that's the community in which I served and in which I now teach. That's where I come from. I also run a Special Forces mentoring group for the young, up-and-coming Special Forces medics in the course. My goal is to help them be less jacked-up than I was when I first got to a team. Another guy and I have been doing that since 2018. I think between the two of us, we've only missed maybe three times in four or five years; I really take that community and commitment very seriously.

And it's crazy, but I'll get a phone call from, say, Romania, and it's some Special Forces medic who has a question. Honestly, I'm the last person anybody needs a call to ask medical advice, but it really does make me feel good when somebody calls me and asks for it.

I can usually answer their questions, but if not, I can at least send them away to somebody who can, but I do take it very seriously. In 2013, I started working on a presentation I would give at the end of the two-week med refresher course I teach. Over the years, it's increased from thirty minutes to two hours. And for every two-week med refresher course, I'm the last guy that they hear. I get guys all the time calling me, texting me, or emailing me and saying, "Hey, I messed up," or "Hey, a guy on my team's messed up. How can you help me fix them?"

I retired from the US Army seven years ago, but they still let me be a part of that community. I have a Signal chat room that's maxed out at 1,000 Special Forces medics. People ask me questions, but I also ask questions. One time, I responded, "Hey, this is the answer. I'm Mike Jackson, nice to work with you." And one of the best compliments I ever heard was his response. He said, "Everybody knows who you are, Mike. You're the OG of Special Forces medicine." And I was like, "Wow, I don't know if I'm actually the OG; there are plenty other people who have been at it longer than me." But that felt good.

That ages me a lot, and I know that sooner or later I have to grow up. I will probably have to leave here and do something better for me. When I have to cross that line, it's going to be a rough. I can't do this forever; I know that.

I am also involved in some local communities. I work with a Boy Scout group out of Columbia, SC, which is about two and a half hours away. I met a guy who was a physical therapist at a wilderness medicine course, and his son was an Eagle Scout in that group.

All the Boy Scout leaders need to be wilderness and remote-first aid-certified through the American Red Cross. Boy Scouts can also attend that course. I run those courses about three times a year as needed for everybody on the south end of North Carolina and the north end of South Carolina in about a two-and-a-half-hour bubble. There is a small Boy Scout camp called Camp Coker in South Carolina, and we usually run it out there. It's a beautiful spot with a big lake and lots of land.

I used to volunteer for the American Red Cross teaching classes for them, but they're a really weird organization. They would rather pay an instructor to teach classes for them than to have somebody volunteer to teach those classes for free. They stopped having any kind of volunteer teach any classes out of my hometown for the American Red Cross, and all they do is pay instructors to teach classes. I don't do this because I want the money; I do because I want to help people save people's lives.

Last week, I had the pleasure of going down to Key West to help with a combat-wounded-vet dive challenge. I was the dive master and dive medical technician for them, and I got to work with some of the most awesome people ever. Over half the participants were missing at least one leg, but nothing slows them down. Nothing. Every now and then, I get to do really special events like that.

I also help with Kinetic Adventure Medical Education, run by two Air Force retired aerospace doctors. And I teach jungle and dive medicine for them. I also have helped them out by teaching for the last three years at the Aerospace Medical Association's conference.

This fall, I will teach at a physical therapy conference because one of my buddies is a physical therapist. They're pushing an outdoor theme, so I'm helping him teach a wilderness medical abbreviated course for some physical therapists. I do pretty much anything outdoors.

I currently don't do much community stuff that isn't work related. I actually decided that I needed another graduate degree, so I'm working on an Austere Critical Care graduate degree. It's funny because in August of 2014, I spent a month up in DC at the Department of Defense Traumatic Brain Injury

Clinic because I had been blown up. Now, I'm working on the same degree that the professionals had who worked on me.

I find that when I push myself and put myself in learning mode, everything works better in my head. My cognition is better, and my memory is better. I get better sleep when I exercise my brain because it's essentially a muscle. It works better, just like a regular muscle.

My main advice for the reader is to find your passions and use your passion to help others. I think there's too much selfishness in our society today. Maybe it isn't always selfishness, but too many people have blinders on. When everything's more expensive, people must work harder and longer just to get the basic essentials. I think people are so focused on getting up, going to work, coming home, and then running around to keep themselves busy that they don't stop to look around and see who they can help.

About Mike Jackson

Mike Jackson is a 3x International bestselling author 3x bestselling author and brings more than thirty years of operational, consulting, and technical experience to The Strategic Advisor Board. Specializing in revenue cycle management, he has acquired a unique skillset that encompasses systems analysis and design, staff training and development, leadership management, and much more.

Mike has more recently focused on strategic consulting services around provider relationships in the healthcare industry. His experience also includes developing and implementing policies and procedures, enforcing leadership standards, and assisting clients in implementing quality programs. Given his depth and breadth of expertise, he is also a regular facilitator and guest speaker at regional, national, and international healthcare conferences.

Mike also consults for the Department of Defense where he is the go-to advisor for all Special Operations training in the medical field and one of the senior advisors to the Special Operations community on all things medical.

THE $80,000 DROPOUT

ALEXIA KAZ

My initial goal in life was to play soccer. I was a Division 1 soccer player, and that was my path ever since I committed to playing pro soccer.

I started playing soccer at an early age and continued through high school. I knew I would be recruited, and soccer was my life. But despite my focus on the world of soccer, I have always been an entrepreneur and interested in entrepreneurship.

I've been reselling on eBay since 2013, so it's been almost ten years. I started when I was only nine years old. I've always been in the entrepreneurship space, but soccer was how I spent most of my time, and it was the joy and love of my childhood.

But when I went to college, soccer was no longer joyful. I had always told myself that I would play soccer until I didn't enjoy it anymore, and I stopped enjoying it when I got to college. I dropped out, and I started my online business, AK Infinite.

I started AK Infinite about a year ago. For the first couple of months, as when building any business, we were focused on setting the foundation and things like filing the LLC, building the website, and building all the back ends.

I really didn't start seeing money come in or getting clients until about two or three months after that. And even after I got my first client, we had to refund him because our system went down in terms of the offer that we were helping him with, and he was flexible, but I value relationships with my clients. Therefore, I decided to refund him until we knew one hundred percent that it would come back. And it ended up coming back a couple of days after that, but I still didn't want to sign him up to then refund him again. However, that's also a great example of what my business mantra is in terms of valuing long-term relationships and valuing the relationship with the client over everything else.

Infinite comes from my first tattoo, which is the infinity symbol. And this also ties into soccer because I look back on when I was around the age of sixteen and getting recruited in soccer, and I just laugh because how was I supposed to know what I wanted to be or where I wanted to be in college and beyond.

I was so young, but during that process, I saw this symbol, and it really connected with me about trusting that I have infinite potential and infinite energy, that I have the infinite power to do anything I put my mind to.

It has many layers of meaning to me, and it's multifaceted in that way, but it's a great reminder of the infinite potential or power that I have, my teammates have, and my team members have in terms of accomplishing anything they believe in and put their mind to. Overall, that's why I chose the name for AK Infinite.

AK Infinite is a full-service digital marketing agency, but we really emphasize online presence, and our main offer is PR. We also do SEO, and I've seen a lot of success with that as well. But PR is an umbrella that includes podcasts, billboards, interviews, but we really value long-term relationships, as well as building client companies and online presence.

Our objective is to have our clients be seen as the authority in their industry. And instead of them doing self-promotion and saying how good they are, we strategize by having other highly credible media outlets speak highly on their behalf. So, we leverage that versus them doing self-promotion.

And, you know, I'd say the why is because it has the perfect balance of being profitable and scalable, while also connecting with people, and those are the two best pillars that I see in a business.

I loved soccer so much because of how connected I was to my teammates and coaches and the sense of community that it brought to my life. And I intentionally bring that connection into my business with my team, as well as my clients, so I see the perfect balance.

And I've learned that soccer and business are mutually beneficial. I don't think I would be as dedicated or committed to my business if it wasn't for soccer.

I was the captain of our club and learned a lot of great leadership skills. I started to see that you could approach some players with your arm around them, and others, you could be a bit harder on them. Just like I can imagine teachers are with their students. And maybe parents are with their kids because not every person, teammate, student, or colleague is the same. So, I learned how to have a balance of perspective with my teammates as well as team members and business.

I decided to attend the University of San Diego to play soccer, but I dropped out after a year. This was a big decision because tuition was $80,000! Part of that was covered by an athletic scholarship, fortunately.

One of the main reasons why I left San Diego, where I went to play soccer, was because I really did not connect with the leadership there. And that is everything to me. It's why I loved and love soccer, and why I wanted to play. But eventually, that wasn't there anymore, and I knew what I didn't want, and I took that knowledge into my business.

In 2018, we were playing in the National Cup. We were in the tournament, and we were doing well, and we kept climbing the rankings. And then we were in the championship game for our age division for SoCal. We had scored in the first half and were up 1-0 at halftime.

With about fifteen minutes left in the game, they got a free kick and scored, tying the game at 1-1. If we remained tied at the end of the game, we would end up in overtime. When there were only eight minutes left in the game, I remember how exhausted I was. We all were. I had been playing the whole game and did not want to go into another fifteen minutes of overtime. It's mentally exhausting more than anything.

I told myself, *We're not going into overtime.* I knew that my teammates didn't want to go in overtime. We kicked off after they scored, and we get a shot right away. Now, there's probably five minutes left. But again, we're attacking, we're doing well, and we're keeping the momentum on our side.

One of my teammates kicked the ball and fumbled a bit, but it came right in front of me, and I shot it right in the bottom left corner of the goal and scored. We ended up winning the game by one point!

Since we won that game, we won state, and we got to go to regionals in Hawaii. Most of us had never been to Hawaii, and we wanted to win state, but we also wanted to go to Hawaii. And with that goal, we won.

It was probably the best goal I ever scored, not because of how pretty it was, but because of where it led to—Hawaii. It was one of the best moments of my life. It is truly amazing to lift others up to that next level, and that's what I hope to continue to do in my business as well.

Overall, the biggest lessons I learned from playing soccer were about leadership and understanding. In soccer, you have different teammates, different team members, and they respond differently. And in terms of community, you must have an open mind, and remember that not everything is black and white, not every person on your team in business has the same life. And there is a sense of balance in that.

Community means everything to me. It is one of the most important aspects of my life in addition to family. But my family is part of my community and close-knit friendships. My soccer teammates were also part of my community.

And I am intentional about who I bring into my community or inner circle, and I'm intentional because of how important that is. Who you surround yourself with is incredibly valuable.

Since my business is fairly new, I'm still working on building that strong sense of a larger community. I'm hoping to start a Facebook group this year, maybe even this quarter. That's something that I'm building into.

We also have an email list. We have an email campaign and send out emails to prospects. But we also have current clients that we keep in touch with via email and follow up with more directly. And I still value building those relationships.

I love the personal touches. I've created hats to give to all my clients once they sign. I'll also give them to my family and friends because it's a reminder like, "Hey, you're part of the AK Infinite family."

In terms of building the Facebook group and community in general, I want the emphasis to be on relationships. AK Infinite is the name and what we're promoting as a business, but relationships will be the focus. It's important for small businesses and businesses of any kind to have a well-oiled machine and solid business model. My team is still planning and strategizing the specifics of how to do that in terms of engagement.

I've been reading a lot of Tim Ferriss lately, and I really love his stuff, especially *The 4-Hour Work Week*. Overall, I like his focus on building a sense of community.

I think we'll also do weekly emails, and my overall plan is just to continue to engage with my clients. It's still a work in progress, but those are the key components that I plan to focus on.

I'm also involved in the Strategic Advisory Board. I got involved with that because I reached out to Jason when we were prospecting. And he wrote me a great email. He knew a lot about PR and the differences between earned media, paid media, and owned media. He's very educated in that. His email was direct that he was only interested in earned media, and if we couldn't deliver that, then he wasn't interested. And he kind of ended it like, "No one really answers this email."

But I appreciated how direct he was. And I always answer my emails in terms of prospect responding, so I wrote him back, thanked him for his transparency, and let him know that I was interested in doing earned media as well. He said I was the only one who responded in that way and said that I was a unicorn, so we hopped on the phone the next day and continued the conversation from there.

Regarding moving forward, I also love to travel and meet new people. I think that can help build your community as well.

It also helps us to learn and stay open minded because we can meet people from different walks of life.

I speak Spanish and am learning Italian right now. It is such a rich experience to be in a different country and culture and speak the language.

Moving forward, I will continue to travel and live into the title of my book, *College Dropout to Digital Nomad.* This is another reason I really enjoy this business model because I can travel and still work on my company. I'm going to Bali in August, and I'm so excited about that.

In terms of goals for AK Infinite, I want to continue to scale it and grow it. That's why I really liked this business model. I'll always do eBay, and I'm still doing it. And I love it. It's something my aunt, and I have been doing since I was nine, but it's not that easy to scale, and it's more challenging versus my current business model for AK Infinite.

With my marketing agency, I'm going to scale it and continue to scale it. I will always do eBay because it's a passion, and I love to do it with my aunt. But in terms of AK Infinite, I want to continue to grow it to the point where I am out of the day-to-day administrative stuff. That was one of the first things Jason told me to do.

It sounds cliche, but I really believe that the power of belief, and the belief you have in yourself is all that matters in terms of making things happen. Of course, there are other factors, and life happens. But believing in yourself is the biggest asset you can have in life and business. And that's what I'm continuing to see and work on.

Another thing that I've learned is that you don't have to stick to the same plan that you once thought you should forever. Leaving school and soccer was one of the hardest decisions

I've ever had to make, and it made the future unknown and incredibly scary. But I'm so grateful I took that leap!

Overall, believe in yourself and continue to build that muscle. With consistency, that will pay off in dividends. And that helps you to be flexible and brave and move into the future more confidently.

About the Author

Alexia Kaz is a former Division 1 soccer player turned digital nomad. College life wasn't for her as she didn't last long there! Putting all her energy into her business, she now runs a successful digital marketing agency out of Los Angeles, CA.

Learn more about Alexia Kaz at akinfinite.com.

The Business (and Community) of CBD

Melanie Kossan

My business is called Mountain Mama LLC. That's the big "corporate" name. It just started out as Mountain Mama Body Butter.

I started five years ago, in 2017. I made body butters, sugar scrubs, and general self-care products. I was selling them locally at farmer's markets. But it very quickly came to my attention that something was going to have to be different about my product to stand out from the rest.

I knew a little about CBD. I did some research, and I began to add CBD to my products. That was in late 2017.

A lot of people kind of get a little of a question mark in their mind about that because the 2018 farm bill wasn't signed until December 2018. How was I adding CBD a year earlier? The misconception is that the 2018 Farm Bill made CBD legal. CBD was already legal, provided that it was imported. The Farm Bill clarified the definitions of Cannabis and Non-THC Hemp, authorized US growers to produce Non-THC hemp, removed Non-THC-hemp-derived products from the DEA's list of Schedule I drugs, and moved regulation for Non-THC hemp from the DEA's office to the USDA.

I was importing full spectrum CBD distillate from Europe. It was very expensive, and a lot of people didn't know about it. But that was why I was doing it. CBD was what made my product different.

It was going to not only be an avenue of self-care because it hydrated the skin and helped you be intentional about self-care, but it also could alleviate some pain and inflammation in your joints and muscles.

I was only doing topicals at the time; tinctures were not widely produced. So, I began immediately. I wanted to grow the company.

I knew that I wanted to get into stores as a wholesaler, but I had to figure out how. I would have to go to a more progressive area because I knew that Billings wasn't ready. I went west to Bozeman. Not only did people not know what I was selling, but I was kicked out of stores because people's misconceptions caused them to believe that I was trying to convince them to sell something that was illegal in their stores.

At that point, it was around the beginning of 2018. I knew that education was needed. Education was the key to this industry. So, I created something called CBD School.

I would go to Billings every month and host a seminar. And I had a presentation, and people would come and pay to listen to me talk.

I would teach them all about cannabinoids: What is CBD? What isn't CBD? How is CBD beneficial in our lives? How can you use it? Why would you use it?

And then, in the end, I would have an opportunity for them to buy product. This helped me sell a lot of products, and it was becoming very popular.

I only had twelve seats, and it would sell out every month. I did it for about the rest of 2018, and the industry locally began to change. With the signing of the 2018 Farm Bill in December 2017, a lot of other people began doing education as well, and I had some authority because I wasn't just the lone CBD peddler anymore.

People were hearing about CBD from other resources as well, and I was simply providing someplace local where they could go and listen about CBD and ask questions, somewhere they could talk to somebody in person about it.

People like to have conversations, even though so many things these days are online. And if you have a question about anything, you just "ask Google." However, people still do like to communicate in person and ask questions.

And when you learn about one thing, sometimes it sparks other questions as well. And that is not something that gets satisfied on Google. There's never going to be any replacement for in-person communication.

Additionally, I went on the radio station in Billings every month and did a live question-and-answer session and answered a lot of questions, sold a lot of products, and was able to get into stores. Simultaneously, tinctures were becoming more popular. Customers would come to me and ask if I had tinctures.

So I began to create them. I've always taken customer feedback and customer requests into account when making new products. I always knew that my products needed to be more potent and purer than anybody else's. So, I never did make a 300-milligram or a 600-milligram tincture.

I do make a 600 milligram for pets who weigh less than 50 pounds. But since CBD dosing is largely weight based, and no people who were taking CBD weighed less than 50 pounds, I started at 1,000 milligrams or higher.

When you're taking your CBD, you must take it regularly; consistency is key. And making sure you have enough is also key.

I've had a lot of people come into my store or my mall kiosk and say, "Oh, I've tried CBD, and it didn't work for me." Inevitably, 100% of the time, if they were willing to try a stronger product like mine, they would always come back and say, "Wow, this was different. This really did help!"

And 100% of the time, it was because it was a stronger product and had more cannabinoids in it.

At the beginning of the company, education became very, very important. And it's remained an important piece of what we do. The original CBD School is available online as a free webinar, and CBD School 2.0 is now out.

We have a huge line of CBD products that we make for people and for pets. We have ingestible products as well as topicals. We have bath bombs, bath salts, healing balms, and all kinds of products. We sell them online and in our store.

And for a period of two and a half years, I had a kiosk in the mall in Billings, and that was very popular. And then COVID happened, the mall shut down, and my kiosk shut down.

It happened two weeks prior to that, and we finally moved the production of the product out of my house and into an actual facility where I had a product production area, a retail area, and my office. And we still have that location to this day. We call it "HQ," and it has served well.

During COVID, businesses all had to close. I had just opened my headquarters two weeks before, and it was very, very important to me that I keep my open sign on. There were businesses that were allowed to stay open. And I had to figure out how I could be one of those.

I spoke with my local health department and discovered that if I was carrying something that was deemed essential, such as hand sanitizer, I could remain open. So that's what I did.

I produced gallons and gallons of hand sanitizer. I donated gallons because the supply chain was very broken. It was destroyed. Everybody was completely depleted of any kind of hand sanitizer and face masks, so everybody was making face masks.

I had a place to make it. I had resources o for buying the supplies to make it. It was still difficult, but it was easier to buy the supplies to make sanitizer than it was to buy sanitizer.

I made the sanitizer, and I donated gallons and gallons of it to people like first responders and nursing homes. Another organization was putting together some care packages for nurses at our local hospital, and I donated personal-sized sanitizers.

Even though I wasn't selling the sanitizer, I was making it available. I would let my local community here know that if they brought in their empty sanitizer bottle, they could refill it for free.

I don't even remember how much I went through. I probably made about 100 or so gallons of sanitizer. Although 100 gallons doesn't sound like much, when you consider the fact that my community only has about 2,000 people, it was a lot.

I was able to keep my open sign on. And, of course, I would also sell some CBD here and there, but mainly, I was really becoming welcomed into my community. Because now I wasn't only there to sell stuff; I was also there to care for my community, which is an essential piece of my overall business plan.

CBD is so great for so many things. And people really can live better lives if they're using CBD at a strong enough dose, a strong enough product of CBD, and using it consistently. It really can help people live better lives.

After COVID, we stopped making the sanitizer because supplies of sanitizer were coming back, and I moved back into my lane of CBD.

Too often, people are afraid to pivot, and I'm like, "Holy moly, pivot!" This is my thing—pivoting. I never had any intention of maintaining the sanitizer thing; I just wanted to keep my doors open, and it worked.

Additionally, it garnered me some credibility in my community because it showed that I am a genuine person and am genuine about my products.

Another major difference between Mountain Mama products and many other CBD products is that we have zero THC in ours. There are a couple of reasons why we stick to zero THC.

One is because almost everybody who has a job locally must have a drug test. They either work for the mine, a refinery, drive truck, or something similar, and they must do a DOT test. Many locals are in law enforcement or the medical community, and they must be able to pass a drug test to keep their jobs.

That's a big deal. People will decide whether they'll take a product based on the fact that they have a career that is very important and provides well for their family and provides benefits, and nobody's going to risk that so that they can take CBD.

Once the United States began to grow more and more hemp, the extracts became more widely available in the States. And they were, of course, a lot more cost-effective to buy in the States.

I wanted to buy in Montana because we've always been loyal to locally produced products and made sure to get as many of my supplies and ingredients as I could from my home state. But it took some steps.

At that time, Montana was growing more hemp than any other state in the country. Now, it's Texas. But in the beginning, Montana was leading the pack.

We still have a lot of growers, mainly in the middle of the state, because hemp grows the best in soil where grains grow the best, such as wheat, hay, or alfalfa. They like the same kind of soil. We have something called a golden triangle right in the middle of our state. And that's where most of the country's feed grain is grown.

I am now sourcing all my cannabinoid extract products from one farm in Alberton, Montana. I love this because I think Alberton's population is around 500 people.

But in Alberton, there is a 16-acre farm that grows hemp, and they provide all the extracts that we use here at Mountain Mama. They're called Mountain Meadow, and they've been a strong partner with Mountain Mama for years.

We were a match made in heaven. I tried out their product, and I got their lab results and read all their certificates of analysis. After a thorough review, I knew they were putting out a great ingredient, and I wanted to be a part of that.

This year, we also started working with other rare cannabinoids, such as CBG and CBN. There is a lot of great information about rare cannabinoids in CBD School 2.0.

In the last year, we have turned Mountain Mama LLC into a corporation that holds two subsidiaries—a distributorship and a podcast. We've also established the CBD Distributors Association, which is dedicated to education and bringing those in the cannabinoid industry together to form a solid industry infrastructure.

We will always focus heavily on education. We use the podcast for education, both ecommerce websites have blogs on them for education, and the association page is all education. We also offer memberships on the association page.

The distributorship is the vending machine arm where we sell small business opportunities for people who desire a passive income. We have these great vending machines that are wrapped in a quality brand and come full of product. We have professionals to advise on the placement of the machines, how to sell ads on your machines, and even financing available. It's truly a no-brainer.

We help your business be successful because when your business is successful, we are also successful.

I always do everything I can to make sure that my products and offerings are top-notch so that people will come and say, "Oh, this product is great!"

Additionally, we do a lot of private labeling. Private labeling is a great way for us to help other businesses be successful. We can make a fantastic product for them, and they can put their own brand on it.

We work with companies who already have a solid following of customers who trust them and value their products and their opinions. When they launch their own CBD line with their label on it, it is always a huge success. It always does very, very well.

We are also working on publishing a print magazine. That will release soon and be published by the CBD Distributors Association. The print magazine will feature others in the cannabinoid industry and how they are benefitting the industry and their communities. This is a great example of other companies supporting other companies in the business community and providing even more education for the consumer.

I interact with many communities. I spend a lot of time interacting with my business community through Strategic Advisor Board and other businesses with my private label programs and my wholesale programs.

However, probably the most important communities I have are my local town community, my association community, and my storefront community. And I think my favorite one is my storefront because, as I said, my storefront is in a very small town.

People who come into my store come in and talk to me about things that they are struggling with. I help them choose a product that can help them to struggle less with that issue.

I go to the grocery store, and I see all these same people. We have a relationship because I have helped them improve their life. And then, in turn, they improve my life by being my customer. And telling their friends about my products. I've also developed many special friendships through my storefront community that I cherish.

But all these same people are my small-town community as well. I am involved in my town by serving on my chamber of commerce board. I serve on other boards as well.

In the spring of 2022, we experienced a devastating flood. This county has never seen a flood like it. And during that crisis, my inner CEO kicked in.

The people who were affected by the flood lived along the rivers, either the Yellowstone River or the Stillwater River. Those who were not affected were desperate to help. For a couple of days, all we could do was watch and pray.

When the water rose, the riverbanks were destroyed. There are no riverbanks anymore. The rivers are no longer where they used to be. They are in other locations, and the entire geography of the county has shifted. New flood zones will need to be established, and maps will need to be updated. You just don't realize all the things that a flood can change. Until it happens.

We lost eleven homes; they just floated down the river. Eighty were seriously damaged, and still others lost acreage that will not be recovered.

The others who suffered most were the ranchers. We're a big ranch community out here in this county, and we have grazing land that's ruined. We lost a lot of fencing, feed equipment, and irrigation ditches.

Amazingly, there was zero loss of life. But for two days, I wanted to know what I could do to help. A lot of these people are my customers, and a lot of these people have become my friends. And I didn't know what to do to help, and nobody knew what to do to help.

There were a lot of people in town who wanted to help, and nobody knew what to do. And I went to local first responder offices and asked what they needed and what people in town needed, and nobody really knew. And I found out that our local government, from the outside, looked like they weren't doing anything.

I decided to put myself in there. I put a plan on paper, and I went into the county office. I spoke with the head of the disaster and emergency services.

And I gave him my plan, and I said, "This is what I'm going to do." And he looked it over; it was both sides of the paper, and he read both sides. And he said, "This is fabulous. I want you to do it, and whatever you need to in this office, it's available to you." From then on, it just grew legs. I ended up organizing volunteers. I've collected an incredible number of donations. I've been to every site in person to see the damage and the destruction. I've cried with people and prayed with them. And I've sat with them while we watch the river literally run through their homes.

The only reason that I was able to organize, coordinate, and help in that situation is because of the way that my business has been structured and the things that I have learned about running a business and being a CEO. I don't have any "formal" education beyond high school. I don't have any degrees in business. I don't have any degrees in horticulture or any degrees in anything.

I've learned everything that I know as I go. I love learning. I love listening. I love telling people about the things that I've learned. And the way that my business is structured has taught me how to take charge of a certain piece of this situation and help the community.

It helped me take important things that needed to be done off the plate of the government so that the government could do the government's job. They were working very hard with state officials and county officials and focusing on assessing the damage and bringing in help from FEMA and other state and federal agencies. But there was a void with the people who were affected.

I'm very intentional about not using the word victim. In my mind, being a victim is a choice. Whether you're going to be a victim depends solely on your mentality. You often hear that word in this area. Almost everybody uses the words "flood victims." I do not use that term. I say, "Those who are affected by the flood."

I owe my CEO skills largely to the Strategic Advisor Board. I've been working with the Strategic Advisor Board for a little over a year at this point. I don't think the same way that I did when I first met Jason Miller.

This is a funny little side story, but as it turns out, I have had a wholesale customer for about three years who sells my product over in the Paradise Valley. And they've loved the product all along. And then, a year ago, I started working with Jason, and as it turns out, they're related.

So today, another guy comes in, and his last name is Miller. I said, "I know Miller is a very common name, but I have to ask you." And I asked if they were related, and he said yes. And I told him why I was asking him, and he's like, "Yeah, it's a small world." It's funny.

The Strategic Advisor Board was responsible for molding the way that I see things with the big picture. And the way that I look at things from a bird's-eye view now instead of down in the muck.

I was down in the muck for the first two days, not knowing what to do. And once I put my CEO hat on, I knew what to do. And I could also help other people who didn't know what to do help.

Another thing I learned during this whole thing is how much I love Montanans. I love Montana because Montanans are very independent and headstrong. I, too, am very independent and headstrong. We mesh well.

When you go up to an 87-year-old man who is a fourth-generation Montana rancher and gingerly working with his tractor trying to put his sandbag wall back up that the river had knocked down again, and you say, "What do you need?" He'll say, "I don't need anything." When from the outside, clearly, he needs something.

But Montanans don't need; we take care of ourselves and each other. We just do what we need to do.

Furthermore, I learned that I needed to communicate differently with this community of people who were affected by the flood. If I approached them and asked, "What do you need?" They would say "nothing."

But when I approached them and said, "What are you struggling with today?" They would tell me what they were struggling with. And that's how I could find out what they needed.

I communicated that realization to all my volunteers and said, "Try very hard not to use the word need because nobody needs anything, right?" And they all understand. "But they do struggle," I told them, "and they are willing to talk with you about what they're struggling with."

In the last two weeks, I have learned so much about who my community is, the geography of my community, the former geography, and the new geography of my community.

Our biggest employer here is a Stillwater Mine. The flood took out the road to get to the mine, which meant that none of the miners could go to work. The mine has been incredible about aiding wherever they can. They get tons done very quickly because they're private.

The best thing about mine is that even though they were shut down, they continued to pay their workers, and the miners were available and willing to help. They were the ones who did a lot of hard labor, like building and moving sandbags.

They all have big trucks. And so we go over to the sandpit, the sand pile where there are sandbags. And they will have fifty people over there filling sandbags and loading them onto trucks.

One of the ways that I was able to help was that I went to the local grocery store, and I got a bunch of snacks, food, water bottles, and oranges. I took them over to the sand pile because all those people had been there all day filling sandbags.

Nobody took breaks. They were working hard. They were filling sandbags all day—mineworkers, their wives, their children, local residents, moms and dads and kids—all of them. They were filling sandbags, and it was one of the most beautiful things I've ever seen.

My brother and I went to the grocery store, and we bought a bunch of stuff. We said, "Here, here it is." We knew that no one would stop to take it, so we just laid it strategically around the sand pile. Sure enough, I went back later, and they had taken it, refueled, re-hydrated, and they were able to continue and do the things they needed to do.

Being immersed in my community and knowing how they work and what their struggles are is very important to me. I did this without even thinking. It just happened.

In order to help your community, all you have to do is walk up to somebody, introduce yourself, and ask them how they're struggling. "How are you struggling today? What can I help you with?" That is all I did. Normally, you wouldn't just freely walk around on somebody's property. That would really get you into trouble and fast. But when there's a disaster, those kinds of things go away.

I just drove around, walked up to houses, introduced myself, and expressed empathy. And I would say, "I am so sorry that you're experiencing this devastation. I'm putting together some volunteers. And these are the resources we have available. And I'd really like to help you connect with that."

And people were very, very receptive. In order to help, you simply must talk to people with kindness and respect. Not one person has turned me away. It is deceptively simple but powerful.

The first day, when I saw the elderly man and his friend trying to rebuild that sandbag wall, I was a little ginger about approaching them. I really had to pep-talk myself into it. However, it wasn't really that scary. And it was just the best thing; I'm so glad I did, and I'm so thankful that what I've learned through the Strategic Advisor Board and Jason Miller has not only helped me be more successful in business but also changed my life and community.

It's 2022, and we do everything on Zoom. We do everything on our phones and computers. But none of that can replace our local communities. Community is personal interaction; it's face-to-face.

Real life provides warmer versions of conversations; it allows you to care about people and learn about people. It allows you to hear people's stories. Everybody has a story. Some people have lots of stories. And sometimes, they lose power through technology. You learn a lot and connect more deeply when you experience people in person.

About the Author

Melanie Kossan; founder, owner, and CEO of Mountain Mama LLC; was born and raised in a military town near Death Valley, California. A lifelong entrepreneur and natural healthcare advocate, Melanie initially began Mountain Mama Body Butter in the fall of 2017, and since then, Mountain Mama Body Butter has morphed into Mountain Mama LLC, which wholly owns its subsidiaries, Stillwater Hemp, All Natural Topicals, and Stillwater Distributors.

Mountain Mama LLC manufactures many kinds of CBD products and markets to wholesale and private-label clients. Stillwaterhemp.com and allnaturaltopicals.com market these products directly to the consumer via e-commerce and our store fronts. Stillwater Distributors offers a passive income to those who wish to get a piece of the CBD market through a licensed distributorship.

Melanie is also founder and president of the CBD Distributors Association, cbdda.org. The Association serves to provide reliable educational information along with establishing and normalizing the cannabinoid industry as a separate industry from the cannabis industry.

Learn more about Melanie Kossan at stillwaterhemp.com.

Communication and Community

Shelby Jo Long

I am the CEO of Business Dynamics. I'm also CEO of Rogue Publishing Partners, which is a consortium of service providers in the publishing industry who help people independently publish their books. And I'm also the Senior Vice President of the Strategic Advisor Board.

I work with businesses to develop additional monetary streams, which could include programs, courses, high-ticket coaching, or any different stream of income that is centered around the expertise in their business. I help people create webinar series as well. I also work with businesses on their culture and communication, internally, and how that presents to an audience externally in their brand.

My "why" comes down to a few things. First, my foundation is in the human communication world, and I have been a college professor in business communication and all things human communication centered for fifteen years. I have a real desire and passion to learn and talk about communication and how we connect with other people. That's what I do within my classes. I like that immediate connection.

I also have this affinity with argumentation and debate. My why, as far as that's concerned, is that I love the debate community because it helps you develop and perpetuate your skills. It's an art form. There's a great community that surrounds debate. It also is a professional community that helps you become better.

My big why is centered around communicating with other people. It also involves engaging with other people, whether it's on an educational level or in a conversation. I love the human connection. Essentially, it all comes down to communication and human connection.

Community is created around language and sharing a common meaning, which has everything to do with connecting with other people on an emotional, logical, and authority level, but that happens in a community. It can't happen unless you're speaking the same language, have similar goals, and share the same values. That's what it centers around. So that connection, the community connection, happens through communication.

Community plays a few different roles within my business. I like having an internal community and then focusing on an external community. I'll explain what those two things are and the differences in them, but it's all about collective problem solving and making sense to your audience.

The internal communities I work with are within Business Dynamics (my company), the Strategic Advisor Board, and Rogue Publishing Partners. I enjoy communicating with other people who have different backgrounds and interests and goals in their organization and businesses. We come up with collective solutions that are better for the organization as a whole, and that is the way I've always operated as far as a business is concerned.

And that comes back to my educational background. I've worked in communities and on teams in the debate world, and in the intercollegiate debate world. But I also have that same approach in my classes. I think that's important because it's a collective knowledge and a collective consciousness that creates better solutions for clients and better solutions for people involved with it.

Additionally, communities focused on internal problem solving give more agency to the people who are involved with them. Therefore, there's more buy-in, and there's more involvement on that side. It's important to have that.

It can be challenging for CEOs of businesses because they make a lot of decisions, but if you're surrounded by a trusted community, then you're not going to make those decisions in a vacuum. You will have that feedback loop that is so critical. When I work with clients, I talk about how important it is to have that trusted internal decision-making structure in your business.

I define your external community as the way a business creates relationships with clients—potential clients, current clients, or past clients. I believe that community is perpetuated by communication, but it's also established by how you and your brand define yourself to the external audience.

If you think about the initial stages of marketing your business or marketing your idea to an audience, how do you emotionally connect with clients or potential clients? What problem do you solve for this potential client? You're probably not the only one out there; there's usually a community of them. Therefore, creating an external community has everything to do with your brand, your goals, and your aspirations as a business.

You can create that external community that's going to support your business. The impact of having that type of external community will be huge, and you can create that in several different ways, anything from a Facebook group to a LinkedIn group to a loyalty program.

If you're running a coffee shop or something local, you create a community that's loyal; you create a community that will always support you, no matter what pivots or changes you make in your business. And you create an external community that's going to be your business support when things get tough or when things get better. It's keeps adding to your business.

Overall, community plays a few roles in business. Those are the two areas that I see as the most important.

I also love masterminds. I love the idea of having a mastermind community of people in my own program, which I use to help people develop curriculum or programs from their expertise. I find it to be extremely valuable to talk to people who are doing the same thing because of that same important idea of having a feedback loop within your community, a critical audience that helps move your program or ideas into the next phase. These help to validate your ideas.

In my career in academia as a college debate coach and a communication professor, I created a few debate programs. I wouldn't call them debate programs; they were more argumentation education programs. There are so many benefits of participating in debate, whether it's developing your speaking skills and increasing your critical thinking skills or learning how to work as a team and adapt to audiences. There are so many benefits of debate but participating on a team requires structure and someone needs to be the head of that structure. Therefore, leading those programs is a labor-intensive activity.

However, I took all the fluff out of the debate community. I broke it down into only the important pieces of debate— making an argument, standing in front of an audience, and working as a team—and turned them into a classroom format. I did that in a couple of different locations.

We created this community in the tribal college debate program that I established in Montana. There are six tribal colleges in Montana, and we engage four of them in this program where I teach traveling workshops. I started creating this community within the classroom, and then they all became part of a broader community in the Tribal College Debate Program.

I also did that in debate camps all over the world. I created my own program in Morocco at a couple of universities there. It's very similar to the tribal college debate program but we had to strip out the debate team part of it. I brought it down to the debate exercises that we did in the classroom, and we created a community around that.

Those are two examples where I did it in academia, but that's one of my teaching methods as well. I use this method in my classes or when I teach small group communication or any communication activity because you'll be involved in groups and teams in any career you're in. Therefore, it's important to work with other people and understand how to engage different perspectives and different ideas and to be able to come up with those collective solutions. In a sense, I've kind of forced the mastermind group work concept in a lot of different areas.

I am involved in many important communities in business as well, including The Strategic Advisor Board. I would say that's probably the most important business partnership I'm a part of because it's such an incredible collection of experts and businesses that can help serve clients in the best way. But it also has served as a place where I can discover more about businesses and professionals and understand more about how businesses work.

We're not competitors, we're partners, and we elevate each other. It's an amazing thing to be a part of. It's also an incredibly expansive web of professionals that can help you solve problems. It's important to be surrounded by experts, and it's important to be surrounded by a community that is lifting everybody up. That's one of those important partnerships that I'm involved in.

Rogue Publishing Partners is similar. There are six of us on the board, plus we have publishing partners that are involved. We're all in the startup together. It's fun to be able to put all these professionals under the same label and see what kind of power and ideas we have.

Those are two important business partnerships because those types of partnerships give you more access to what the marketplace will respond to, and you have more access to experts who can help guide you through things. Those two are my most important partnerships, but I think it all comes down to the relationships and the impact that you make in the marketplace.

I've been a college professor here at a small local college for sixteen years, but one of the most important and foundational communities that I've been a part of is the intercollegiate debate community. I've been a part of that community as a competitor, but I have also been a coach for over twenty-five years. I have lifelong friends in there. I'm still friends with my debate coach from college, and we're colleagues now, and we share students. It's interesting how that develops.

There's camaraderie in that debate community. It's very competitive, but there's an interesting dichotomy because it's also an area that's full of so much talent that it lifts everybody up. There's a balance of competition and collaboration within that community. That's had a tremendous impact on not only my academic life but also the recovery from my accident, which is another story that I'll get into later, It's good to have that community of lifelong friends and learners that contribute to your career.

If you're a business, and you want to start your own community, look to those who already trust you, and those with whom you already have a business relationship or partnership. That's where you start your community because communities develop on trust, and relationships are the key to community.

When you start with those trusted relationships, other relationships develop from there through the common values or common goals that you might have. Once you discover that core reason for your connection, you can start creating a community around that.

For example, I work with quite a few business coaches to articulate their business programs, and I work with authors to develop high-ticket coaching programs out of the books that they've written. There's always some sort of transformation or journey that a coach and an author try to take their audience through. You focus on the journey and the results of the journey. That's where you start creating your community.

If you are a coach who wants to provide your clients with better health and a better lifestyle and having better relationships, then focus on the results, and build your community around where you're taking your audience. People want to share that vision. People want to share their goals.

That's the fundamental reason that we're in relationships, so we can share that with other people. That's a good place to start. If I'm working with a fitness coach and the goal of fitness is to be in better shape, the journey should impact you and inspire you to be in better shape. You want to fit better in your clothes and feel better about yourself. You must think about those results and build your community around that.

Branding also ties into community because your brand is who you are, who you serve, and what problem you solve. Those are the fundamental pieces of your brand. As I mentioned earlier, the purpose of your brand is to create a brand that is not about a service. A brand is about an emotional connection that you have with an audience and a transformation.

People are loyal to brands because we have an emotional connection to them. I am loyal to one coffee shop because, yes, they have good coffee but so do a hundred other coffee shops, but I also like being there. I like the emotions that I feel when I'm there. I feel welcome, and there are a lot of positive emotions that are tied around that.

The same is true with any service provider in business. If you're an insurance agent, and you sell insurance, there are millions of people who sell insurance. But your brand is what creates the connection with people. It's also what sustains that connection with people and why people will be loyal to your service.

Your brand, and how your brand functions, plays into building community because it connects to groups of people and a target audience when you start marketing your business. There are groups of people who want to experience that transformation, experience that change, and the more emotional connection you have to potential clients, the more they will be drawn to your brand.

From there, it all has to do with loyalty, emotional connection, referrals, and sustained long-term relationships. That's what branding is all about. It's not about a one-time business transaction; it's about doing things. It's about transactions, but it's also about a sustained relationship to sustain through those transactions and to build your business more and to build those relationships more.

That's why an important piece of that brand is that you need to tell your story. And you need to have a personal stake in that because I don't have a relationship with a service, I have relationship with the person who's providing the service.

For example, I've had my insurance agents for fifteen years. I like them. They solve my problems quickly, and we have a long-term relationship. They check in. It's about creating and sustaining that long-term relationship; it's not just about the one-time transaction.

That is the key to building community. That's how we build that external community with our business. We have those long-term clients. We have that group of people to propose new ideas to. Again, your brand is all about an emotional connection to your clients, and you can develop community around that.

My book is called, *I See Your Genius: Transform Your Idea into Income*. There are three different sections of the book. The first part of the book is about my story. The second one is about my transformation into entrepreneurship and my transformation through the entrepreneurship journey. And the third section is about the process I take my clients through.

I'll talk first about community and how important that was for me and the development of my ideas. I had a traumatic brain injury at the end of my junior year of high school. I was in a coma for sixteen days, and then I had recovery after that. Fortunately, I was able to go back to school, finish high school, and then go on to college that following fall.

In the book, I dig deep into why I recovered. I believe it came down to two things: my perseverance and the identity

I had before the accident. I wanted to return to that and be a part of it.

I was also involved in communities before I got in the accident, and those communities became an important piece to rebuilding my identity after the accident. I was on the debate team, and I was in student government. I was involved in several activities and communities, and I attribute a lot of my recovery and the ability to go to college the next year to being on the debate team where I had to speak.

I went to college the following year, and I joined the Carroll College debate team in Helena, MT. I was on that team for four years while I finished my undergraduate degree. That community transformed the way I speak, the way I think, and the way I network. I have a network all over the world because of it.

So, community was very instrumental in my personal life. In my entrepreneurship journey, it's really hard to do it on your own. You need a community. It's hard to find all the answers. Yes, you can read books about entrepreneurship or somebody else's journey, but in the end, it's going to be *your* journey.

This is why it's so important to be part of supportive communities. It's lonely to be an entrepreneur, so you need trusting people and trusting communities to help. If you surround yourself with a community where you can find that help, that support, it makes things a lot easier.

For example, I've been a part of multiple communities and masterminds. I was a part of a local one called Vista Business Network. We were fifteen business professionals who met once a week, and we talked about our businesses. We also had a referral partnership, and we did business development workshops. It was good to have those connections to help build our businesses.

I have also been part of mastermind communities where we talked about the same books, and the same leadership principles, and those communities are important. In the development of your business, and in your entrepreneurship journey, it's important to know you have a community to help you with your challenges.

The promise I make in my book and in my business is to transform your idea into income. It's your idea. It's your expertise. But when you place yourself in a position to coach people through a process, and you are the expert in that process, it's vital to develop a community who is a part of that transformation.

It is important to have that connection of people who are going through the same thing. Whenever we go through any sort of transformation, there's vulnerability to that. There's vulnerability to any change that we make.

Being surrounded by other people and understanding that other people are going through the same struggles and changes, but they're being guided in that process—that community becomes a vital part of your business. Not every business needs to have a coaching program involved with it. Some programs are developed just to make things easier and systematize things. But for that, it's important to have a community that is going through that transformation to help people through their journey.

Community can be found in different places. It's a part of most of what I do, including my involvement is with Rogue Publishing Partners and the Strategic Advisor Board. Those are communities of people who all elevate each other. We all are on a team together. We all have similar goals, we want things to succeed, and we want to grow together and not stay static.

Being in a community makes life much more dynamic and makes solving your problems a lot easier and more efficient than if you're a solo entrepreneur. As far as my book is concerned, a lot of it is community-based because I talk about talking about community and brand and how important that is to developing your business.

Community is central to both building and sustaining your business. It's also central to the longevity of your business, but you can't build community without trust and trusting other people. There are a lot of people who are out there just to make money, and there are a lot of people who are out there to take your money.

When you find that trusted community, then you have the foundation to really grow your business. You have the foundation to make a bigger impact with your business and make a bigger impact with your voice and your transformation. Yes, you can have community, but trust is the next level, and creating a community around people you trust is incredibly important.

I was listening to podcasts the other day, and there was one by a serial entrepreneur in the tech industry. He is constantly developing and loves being in the creative space, but he talked about how he develops businesses. I've talked about this with Jason Miller, the CEO of Strategic Advisor Board. We create communities out of our friends, and we go into business together because we like to hang out with our friends, and we get to talk to our friends more.

The serial entrepreneur on the podcast kept creating businesses so he could be around his friends. I feel like I'm at that place now with Strategic Advisor Board and my community with Business Dynamics. I have a nice team that can help take care of people's problems. And with Rogue Publishing, I needed a community to help develop my book. Overall, community is key and trusting people is the key to making that community function.

About the Author

Shelby is a 3x bestselling author and 3x international bestselling author, speaker, professor and business strategist who helps businesses grow their brand by developing custom programs and courses. She transforms the unique ideas and approaches that experts have developed in their lines of work into a program or course so they can scale their operations.

Shelby's professional background includes fifteen years as a business communication professor and intercollegiate debate coach at a college in Montana. She has taught classes in the human communication discipline, including business communication, public speaking, small group communication, argumentation and debate, persuasion, and organizational communication. Her involvement with debate has enabled her to travel around the US and the world. She has conducted international communication and debate seminars in New York City, Mexico, Bosnia, Ireland, and Morocco. She has also taken students across the US and various countries for international debate competitions.

In Shelby's business coaching and consulting work, she has provided business culture and communication training at state and private organizations. She has also been invited to speak at women's conferences, chamber events, and real estate conferences about leadership, organizational culture, and branding. Her communication and advocacy backdrop gives a unique perspective to how a business communicates their message to their audience.

Learn more about Shelby Jo Long at shelbyjolong.com.

TRIBE + PURPOSE

OTIS MCGREGOR

I grew up in Fort Worth, went to Texas A&M, and joined the Corps of Cadets while there. While I was there, I decided I wanted to get more experience prior to joining the Army, so I enlisted in the National Guard. I spent a little over three and a half years in the Texas Army National Guard as a tank driver and then as a long-range reconnaissance and surveillance patrol soldier.

I got my commission out of Texas A&M as an engineer and took my brand-new, beautiful Texas bride with me to our first duty station in Fort Wainwright, AK, which is right outside of Fairbanks. There's no better way to test the marriage than throwing yourself into the Arctic environment. While there, I raised my hand to volunteer for Special Forces.

After four years in Alaska, I came back to the lower 48 and went through Special Forces training. My Green Beret unit was assigned to Fort Carson, CO, and we spent about four years there. I got to do some amazing missions with some amazing men. Then I had to pay the piper. I spent about two and a half years in DC, paying the price for all the fun I had.

I came back to Colorado (where I still live) and commanded for a couple of years, and then got some experience at the next level at what was the original US Space Command. And then the US Northern Command (USNORTHCOM). From there, we went to Europe, assigned to Special Operations Command Europe, and got to do some very interesting things in standing up a headquarters and building teams there. I came back here to USNORTHCOM and retired from the Army. I like to tell people that's where the wheels fell off.

During my Army career, I had a very clear plan of what I wanted to do. I wanted to be a lieutenant colonel for 20 years and retire. And the only plan I had after the Army was to get a job. And that was poor planning for somebody that should have known better.

I spent the next seven years bouncing from job to job in five different companies. All of them were great companies, but after about ninety days at every one of them, I would get frustrated. My gut would tell me something wasn't right, and after anywhere between six months and eighteen months, I'd quit. I would consult for a little while, then somebody else would offer me a job. I did that for five different companies.

I should have been pretty darn happy at the last company I worked for. I was the Chief Strategy Officer for a small business based in my hometown of Fort Worth, TX. I was good friends with the owner. As Chief Strategy Officer, I had carte blanche to do whatever I wanted, whenever I wanted, and with whomever I wanted because I was doing business strategy, and there's nothing more ill-defined than that. I was the only guy in the company who worked remotely. After eighteen months, even with all that freedom and autonomy, I was still just as frustrated and miserable in that job as I was with every other one.

One summer afternoon, seven years ago, I was sitting in my home office feeling sorry for myself. I started to ponder on who I was supposed to be, what I was supposed to be doing, why I wasn't happy, and things that should have made me happy. As I sat there and reflected on my life post-Army, I realized that since leaving the Army, only two things in my life had been consistent: Number one was my family. I'm still married to my beautiful Texas bride. But number two caught me off guard a little, and that was rugby.

Shortly after I retired from the Army, I started coaching boys high-school rugby. Our youngest son wanted to play rugby, and my wife and I did the typical middle-America thing where she would pick him up from school, drop him off at practice, and I'd leave work and pick him up on the way home. I started leaving work a little earlier and hanging out on the sidelines. Then I started talking to the coach, we became good friends, and he asked me to be to join as an assistant coach.

The next year, he asked me to take over as the head coach. That same summer that I was sitting there feeling sorry for myself, I had just finished my seventh year of coaching. I realized that all throughout those years, I used to tell people the only reason I was working that job for company XYZ—whether it was Lockheed Martin, Armor Global, ISS, you name it—was so it could fund my habit, the thing I really enjoyed, which was coaching rugby.

I looked at what it was about coaching rugby that was really fulfilling for me, and I broke it into three pieces. Number one was the love of the game. I didn't grow up playing it; I was introduced to it when my son started playing. It's an amazing team sport that requires a lot of physicality, a lot of teamwork, and a lot of strategy to be successful.

The second piece of what fulfilled me was the boys. That coaching gave my wife and me thirty-five extra sons in and out of our house. It's a club sport, so our house was the clubhouse, and we loved those boys just like our own.

But the third piece was what I realized was really fulfilling for me, and that was being their coach. It was challenging those young men to do more than they thought they could, holding them accountable, and teaching, mentoring, and guiding them, not just to be better rugby players but better young men and better men in society.

I engaged the next level of my network and started talking to a few friends about what this could mean. I had already made a very conscious decision that I was not going to become a professional rugby coach at the age of fifty. A couple of my friends asked if I had ever heard of leadership coaching, business coaching, or executive coaching. "Nope, never heard of those." The only thing I'd ever heard of was life coaching, and I was not going to be the next Tony Robbins. Plus, I'd met some life coaches at networking events, and they were all these touchy-feely soft talkers. That is not me. But these guys taught me about another way of coaching and that I didn't have to be that guy.

I was introduced to a certified coaching program from iPEC, the Institute of Professional Excellence and Coaching. I signed up for that and tapped into the second and third levels of my network to get introduced to some successful coaches. I bought them cups of coffee and learned how they became successful, how they became coaches, and how they ran their businesses. I took what was then my consulting business, LTO Enterprises, and converted it into a coaching business, and I ran it that way for several years.

I made two more commitments to myself when I shifted my business. The first was to get involved in the Colorado Springs community. At that point, I'd been in and out of the area for a total of fifteen years, between the military and then retirement. All I knew was where my two favorite restaurants and two favorite bars were, so I made a commitment to build my network and get to know my neighbors.

The second commitment I made was to give back to the veteran community, to the veteran tribe, because that's where I feel like I received everything that's made me as successful as I am. I wanted to share all my experiences with these guys so that they didn't experience the same frustration I did when I left the Army with no purpose, no guidance, and no identity. I focused on that, and I work for two nonprofits, The COMMIT Foundation and The Honor Foundation, helping soon-to-be veterans (we call them fellows) create their next adventure in life.

About a year and a half ago, I rebranded my company from LTO Enterprises to Tribe and Purpose, which better fits who we are. We believe that nobody is successful without people around them, their tribe, and it's important to understand your purpose. You need a purpose to know what to do every day so you're not just going through the motions. We're much happier when we live with intention and in control.

A community, in my book, consists of people who are geographically co-located who form a bond with your next-door neighbor, the person across the street, or even the guy you see at the pub. They're all part of your community, and there's some bond there because of co-geographic location, which gives you commonality.

But I like to take it one step further and refer to that as a tribe. The difference between community and tribe is a tribe consists of like-minded people. They have similar values, not exactly the same, but they have to be similar enough so that everyone is comfortable. There's little to no friction, and where there is friction, it's acceptable friction. Everybody in the tribe wants everybody else to succeed. That's an important distinction between community and tribe for me.

When 9/11 happened, everybody came out and lit candles. We felt very close and tight-knit for a couple of days, but then we went back to the same old wave-from-across-the-street sort of thing. The difference in a tribe is that person comes over and checks on you. That's not to say that your neighbors can't be part of your tribe, but to me, there's a line between the community, the geographic community, and a tribe that requires those similar values and a desire to help everybody within the tribe be successful.

My tribe is a network or group of people I love working with to help share what I know so that they can have more success. One of the tribes I have is the Veteran Business Leader Mastermind. I've been doing that one for about three years now. It's a group of eight to ten veterans who get together regularly to celebrate each other's successes and dive in to help each other when we're having problems.

We are authentic enough with each other to share our problems and ask for help. It's not just showing up and nodding your head in agreement, but spending the time, our most precious asset, to help each other succeed. That's what being part of a tribe is. They're a group of people you can call on to ask for help, and they give it to you willingly.

I can give you a quick example. I did a TEDx back at the end of April. My TEDx video was posted on their website and was getting a lot of views. I think it had somewhere between 1,700 and 1,800 views in the first couple of weeks. And then I got a notice from the TEDx organizers that they had to take it down, and not just mine but everybody's video. They said it was due to technical problems.

So, they took my video down from the TEDx channel on YouTube, and then they reloaded it, which meant there was another delay and TEDx had to review the video again. This time, however, they decided that my talk was outside of the parameters and policies of TEDx. They posted the exact same video, but instead of posting it to their YouTube channel, they posted it as unlisted on YouTube with a warning that said my talk violated their policies because I talked about warfare, and some audiences may find that disturbing.

My video now had zero views, so I took the link and sent it to my friends and a couple of veteran groups and asked them if they could help me out. And it exploded. In just ten days, an unlisted video had over five hundred views, over sixty likes, and over twenty comments. That's an example of what a tribe can do and why we need a tribe.

Tribe + Purpose

When people join the Tribe and Purpose community, they become part of a tribe that cares about them. People who don't want to help others and don't want to help others succeed are not a good fit for the tribe. The other thing they get as being part of Tribe and Purpose is clarity in their purpose, in who they are and what their identity is. We teach them how to figure out what their purpose in life is and how to start to live life in pursuit of their purpose.

When members join, there are three steps we do to help them immediately. Step One is helping you understand who you are. You need to know where you're at on the map. No GPS can plan a route to a location you want to go unless it knows where you are at that moment.

So, we give you some tools. We talk about energy, and not in the aura Far East sense, but understanding positive and negative energy and how we show up and how they can make choices in life and understanding that. They start to understand how they can choose to show up either pissed off and blaming people or happy and looking for opportunity. It's a choice we help you understand.

In Step Two, we walk you through an exercise on how to visualize where you want to be and who you want to be. I do this by helping you create the ideal day, five years from today. It's kind of unique, and I've combined several techniques to create this. What's significant is that the more details you put into what your ideal day looks like, the more real it is and becomes.

Not only can you develop a backward plan to get there and create it from today until five years from today, but your subconscious looks for actions to help you achieve that goal. I do it in five-year increments because five years is far enough out that you can accomplish a lot, yet it's not so far out that it feels alien.

There's one other thing that's unique about this that's a bit of a time fallacy. We try to do too much in a day. We always plan for more to get done in a day than is humanly possible. It's a weird mental thing. But we also, in this weird human survival sense, take that same time fallacy and flip it. The things we think will take us five years to accomplish will only take us two or three years. If you're focused on what your vision is, what that ideal day looks like for you in five years, and you truly believe it, it pulls you. There's no doubt in my mind that you're going to bust your ass to get it.

Step Three is to take your vision and help you build the plan. We take that vision and break it down into goals. Goals are those major accomplishments you need to achieve your vision. We then take your goals and break them down into objectives. Think of objectives as those things that you can accomplish in a week or a month. From there, we take your objectives and determine the action steps, the daily tasks that need to be done. *What do I need to do this afternoon that will move me one step closer to achieving my vision?*

So, we get you set on that path. From there, we go back and start asking questions such as, *What is your purpose? If that's your vision, how does your purpose align with that vision?*

Most people are afraid to commit to an ideal day five years from today because they don't want to fail at achieving it. And in the same line, those same people are afraid to commit to a purpose because they think, *If I say that's my purpose, and I find out it's not, then I'm a failure.* It's a really interesting thing that goes on in our minds because if we take that idea of what our purpose could be and walk towards it and we find out it's not, then we just get more clarity on what our purpose may be by realizing *Oh, nope, that's not it.*

And for the people who have zero clue, the ones who don't know who they are and what they want to do, I walk them through understanding what their passions are. I have them do the same thing with their passions that I did when I broke coaching rugby down into those three components.

The way you know if you're passionate about something is you have no concept of time while you're doing it. When you're done doing it, you feel energized and not drained. You feel excited about it. We have people take those things they feel passionate about and break them into the main components, and we do that with three to five passions. We take those three to five passions, and we break each of those up into three to five major components. And what you find when you do that is a trend line.

Let's look at an example of cooking in the kitchen or doing a woodworking project in the garage. Often, you're following a recipe, but you're dynamic in how you follow it. You've got some guidance and some idea, but you're going to be a little flexible with it.

Same thing on that woodworking project in the garage. If you're building a bench and decide you want to do it just a little differently, you're following some guidance, but you're modifying it. I found that it is spot-on for most military folks. They start to see this pattern, this trend line of who they are, and it helps them start to understand what their purpose is.

Your purpose should pull you forward each and every day. You have a vision for the ideal day that aligns with your purpose. Your purpose is your overarching guide, and a purpose cannot be achieved. A purpose can only be fulfilled. A vision is something that is achieved or completed.

I spoke with an amazing woman recently, Coach Valencia Peterson. She started a program called Open Door Abuse Awareness & Prevention, and she goes into inner-city high-school football programs and teaches young high school men how to handle their anger, how to control themselves, and that violence is not right. As a little girl, she saw her father murder her mother, so she has a passion for helping people understand how to control violence. That has become her purpose. That is what she lives for. It pulls her every day, and she's hugely passionate about it.

If your purpose does not pull you, it's not truly your purpose. I'll leave you with a bit of Japanese philosophy from the island of Okinawa. It's called *ikigai*. Ikigai is your true purpose—who you are and what you strive to do. It's a Venn diagram that consists of four components: What are you good at? What do you love to do? What will people pay you for? And what does the world need? And where those four things intersect, that's your ikigai.

What I'm doing right now with my life, with Tribe and Purpose, is I am pursuing my ikigai because I love what I'm doing. The world needs it. I'm good at it. And people pay me to do this. That's ikigai.

Not everybody gets paid to pursue their purpose, but I do, and my purpose is to create a legacy of leaders. I believe that great leaders create great organizations, and great organizations create great communities, and with great communities, we have a better world. That is what drives me to do what I do: give back, share my experiences, help people discover their purpose, and live life with intention.

About the Author

LTC, Special Forces, US Army, Retired Otis McGregor leads Tribe and Purpose with his son Camden. With over 40 years of experience as a leader, coach, and team member, Otis embodies the values and principles of Tribe and Purpose. He has empowered hundreds of businesses and individuals to find their clarity for purpose and their tribes for connection. Otis leverages the unique blend of heart, passion, and experience as one of the elite commanders of Green Berets.

Learn more about Otis at tribe-purpose.com.

Finding Community Everywhere You Look

MIKE OWENS

M y first inkling of earning money was back when I was twelve years old. I remember asking my dad if I could have a stereo, and he told me I had to earn it myself. So, I got a job trying to sell newspaper subscriptions door to door. That gave me my first feeling of earning a dollar, and I wanted to learn how to earn more of that so I could get the things I wanted.

After high school, I went to a community college to get a culinary degree, which I did not finish. My mind is very sporadic, and I'm always interested in just about everything that there is, which really is not good when you're trying to focus on earning money. I had to learn to curtail that type of behavior.

I got into the restaurant industry because I like to be creative, and in culinary school, you have to be creative in order to pull a masterpiece of a product together to get some type of validation of what you've done. So, I went into the corporate world, and I quickly found out that it was too structured for me. It really restricted my entrepreneurial spirit, and I hated the idea of trying to climb that ladder.

I took a plunge, and at the age of twenty-four, I opened a small grocery store. After a year, I realized that I was crazy to be working 24/7 with just three employees. It wasn't sustainable, so I went back into the restaurant industry, back into the corporate world, only to find out that, again, it wasn't for me.

I had to save the money that I needed to start out my first venture, but I also realized that I didn't have enough money to do it right. So, I had to go out there and pitch my business plan to my friends, family, and business owners in order to get my first restaurant open.

I got the restaurant open, but I found out that even when though you think it's a great concept, not everyone is just going to show up because you've opened the doors. I didn't think about having enough capital to foresee how the economy would change or doing feasibility studies or understanding my target market, etc. All those things that I know now but didn't know then were a good learning experience. That being said, I was successful for my first eight years. Then my partners and I parted ways, and I went on to my next venture.

All that experience taught me to stay true to myself and persevere through whatever obstacle there is. I had to learn the business part as I went because I was wet behind the years. I didn't have any formal training or education in business. I had corporate-background experience learning about processes, P&L, marketing, and all that stuff, but it's different when you do it on your own.

I started pivoting about twenty years ago while I had my restaurants. I got involved in consulting more as a side gig to help other business owners see through any issues that they had, and a lot of those clients came through word of mouth through other people and business owners who referred those business owners to me. It was more of a grassroots type of hobby just to help people. That went on for ten to fifteen years.

I got into full-time consulting about three years ago, and transitioning to that came fairly easy for me. Because of my hands-on experience going through the trials and tribulations of opening a restaurant, I seemed to have the ability to understand and help others to see what they're not seeing. And so that transition was easy for me.

Working primarily online is different from a brick-and-mortar business. A lot of planning is required to open a brick-and-mortar business. It takes longer, anywhere from six to twelve months, to get that off the ground. There's a lot more risk involved. You're going to have a certain amount of business come in just because of visibility, but that doesn't mean you're going to be a success in it.

Transitioning into consulting is a little different because now it's all about reputation and word of mouth. You're going out there and making sure that it's sustainable so that you can make a living. You're probably taking a pay cut doing that, which I did because it's a lot different. You're transitioning into a new career, but you're trying to hone skills that are different from what you were doing in a different business setting. It's more about relationship building. You're learning how to talk to people and use the right emotional avatars, if you will, in order to connect with them.

It's different when you're the boss and holding all the hats out there, and anxiety is hitting you every day that you're trying to make payroll for a million dollars. It becomes a little frail but relieving at times when you do that.

Today, I'm the CEO of MACO Consulting Group, which offers results-based consulting that focuses on small-to-midsize businesses from $3 million down that are hospitality or retail or more service-related industries—businesses that have five to thirty employees, maybe even a little larger than that depending on their volume.

We focus on helping them find the gaps in their business and understand what it is that they're not seeing. We work to fix those gaps and help them understand what their goals are to achieve the next level. It's a simple process of putting everything in front of them that they don't see and helping them have an aha moment.

It's really a conversation where they open up and ask questions, and we help them find the answers, or at least help them understand what they're not doing so they can make the right decision to move forward. It's a simple format, and it's fun watching how small businesses grow from the learning experience that they go through with us.

I belong to several communities, some of them quite large, but I've learned not to limit myself to that. I've always felt that one-on-one relationships with business owners are just as important as a large community. A community can be one or many. You can get a lot out of sitting down with a business owner.

I recently drove three hours to Kansas City to have a three-hour conversation, a small mastermind, with a business owner with Dining Alliance. He owns several businesses, and I've known him for years. We bounced off ideas with each other about what we had to offer and how we might be able to help each other. He retired from the corporate world two years ago and transitioned as well, most of it online.

You're going to find, especially in today's world with the pandemic, that there are a lot of people transitioning careers. They are taking their experiences and trying to create a service that helps others.

Most are finding out that it's not that easy to transition into a new career, but once that individual gets into their comfort zone and really focuses on their business, their collective experiences take hold. When trying something new and different, it can really challenge your mind. That's where mentoring programs and communities help. You can't do it all yourself. You need self-awareness to understand that you need help to be able to help others.

Find a community of people you resonate with and who share similar beliefs and ideas. I don't have one particular way of finding community. I just go seek. I network. I go out there and look at what's available and what type of mentoring programs there are.

Some of the avenues I use are online platforms like Alignable, a platform where a lot of businesses get together to bounce ideas off each other. It's not a platform to go sell your business or sell your service or your product; it's a platform to ask questions and help each other.

The American Club Association is another business group along the same lines. You don't sell to each other. It's more local and regional. It's something I haven't fully benefited from because it's hard for me to get away, but it's a good resource to connect with other businesses.

I'm also in a mentoring program. You can be either a mentee or a mentor. I was recently listening to a mentor, April Sabral. She's the founder and CEO of RetailU and the author of *The Positive Effect: A Retail Leader's Guide to Changing the World*. She's very passionate about positive leadership and its impact on businesses. She believes that leadership can make or break a person, not just a business, and the impact of positive leadership can ignite the best in people. I feel the same way about that.

You can go online or get involved with the local business chapters within your own community. As I sit here and think about it, my mind is going crazy with all the different ways to find community. I don't think there is one single magic bullet. It's important to understand who you are and the message that you want to give.

Once you understand what you're trying to achieve in helping people in other businesses, then you align yourself with those groups and those communities that will best serve your needs, whether it be one business owner or a business group, in your community or online.

As the saying goes, "The speed of the leader is the speed of the team." You're always under the microscope, and people will follow you if you take the lead, so it's important to look in the mirror and understand what level of leadership you're at. You don't have people patting you on the back; you have to lift yourself up. To do that, you have to stay positive and be in the right mindset on a daily basis. It's important to be a part of supportive business communities.

About the Author

Michael Owens is a 3x international bestselling author and 3x bestselling author. His experience started in the corporate landscape reaching mid-level upper-management status, leading into creating conceptual businesses in the hospitality and retail space as a partner, owner, and operator for more than thirty years. In that time, he became familiar with what's important in operating a successful operation in terms of driving revenue, operational efficiencies, marketing, business procedures, and ROI.

With his strengths in business strategy, operational implementation, business procedures, and financials, Michael has taken his experience and harnessed this passion to help other business owners and leaders to reach similar heights and beyond. After successfully helping several reach success, he took this motivation to help as many business owners and leaders as he could through his many years of experience.

Learn more about Mike Owens at macoconsultinggroup.com.

mPro—The Ultimate Community Platform

JOEL PHILLIPS

Community and marketing should be intimately connected. First, let's take a look at the challenges that the current marketing environment and big tech have placed on us, especially with retargeting. Retargeting used to be a powerful tool for marketers. Now, big tech is fencing their data; they're putting a wall up around it.

First, Apple changed its default iPhone operating system from opt-in to opt-out in September 2019. What this meant was that Apple had turned off the spigot for retargeting, which is the most valuable piece of marketing there is. From that move, Facebook lost $232 billion in market capitalization—in one day!

When Apple turned off Facebook's ability to track with cookies or pixels, which is Facebook's primary revenue-generating technology, they turned off the ability for retargeting. This made Facebook's advertising go up in price and made their ability to expose ads to consumers go down.

Everyone thought that Apple was the big privacy hero for this move, but in reality, it was just about the money. Not surprisingly, forcing third-party tracking out made Apple's own ad platform usage go way up. Now, Apple has a fence around their data, so nobody, third party or otherwise, can access it unless you opt-in.

If no third party can access it, you can't use cookies, and you can't use pixels. You can't do anything you need to do to track and re-show ads. Therefore, the use of Apple's ad platform went way up because they allow retargeting with their own consumers, but they don't allow other ad servers to do it. Essentially, it's a big data-hoarding process. And Apple has forty percent of the market.

So, we know where Google's going. In fact, they've announced that by the end of 2022 or the beginning of 2023, they will do the same as Apple. And they will turn off the ability for third-party access to cookies and pixel tracking or tracking of any sort unless you specifically opt-in. Remember, this is all in the name of privacy, and Google makes up the remaining 60% of the market

Within their proprietary platforms, you can still retarget—but only within their platform. If you want to serve a Google ad to Google Android users, then you can do that. But only within the Google universe; you can't do it with Facebook or on any other platform. And Facebook is just an example of all third-party tracking in the marketplace.

Facebook is only one example, but to turn it off for everybody means that Google is putting a fence around their data that nobody has access to it except for them. Nobody will opt in because they think that Google and Apple are great privacy heroes—but they're not. It's all about profit. Which is one way that big tech is negatively impacting the marketing world.

How, then, do business owners market? How do they reach consumers? How do they reach anyone?

Communities are now the biggest and best hope for business owners. Communities allow the ability to market within the community because you become a known commodity within that collection of like-minded individuals and companies. If that community is based around marketing, that means the community I reach out to has an interest in marketing, whether it be LinkedIn, email, Facebook, or whatever channel I've developed a one-on-one relationship with. And it is the community that allows me to have that conversation with a consumer versus a cold interaction.

However, if I don't have that cold interaction, where and how can I grow my community base? I must find other ways to grow my collection of followers who will become loyal to my brand. Outreach, blind outreach, has been the primary driver of inbound traffic.

Now, I have to focus on building inbound traffic by using tools other than solely utilizing paid ads to get people to come across my site. All of this is geared to building compelling offers that make people want to interact with my brand, as opposed to interacting with somebody else's brand.

Building inbound traffic by connecting people to your mission is the key. The efficacy of paid outreach alone has been drastically diminished. All of this is to say that the change in focus becomes a change in how we *reach* consumers to how we *attract* consumers.

There are a lot of tools at our disposal for "attracting" consumers but attracting them to a community of like-minded individuals is how you force-multiply your efforts. This makes community a critical marketing component for the near future.

Instead of running ads to target a circle of people, we must now depend on asking companies if they have a circle we can talk to. I have to reach out instead of simply paying for an ad or any other cold outreach methodology. I must now find companies who have an interest in what I do or that might be compatible with a co-branded interest and then reach out to their community.

But how do we do that with all these changes in privacy and big tech? I think there's going to be a conservative, concerted effort for more networking and more business interaction between entities because this big tech hold on data will become untenable at some point.

What happens when Apple has that monopoly on its data? All their prices go up; it's proven. What happens when Google does the same thing? When there's no competition, they can charge whatever they want. And they're already making big bucks. So, it may be a slow burn, but the value will diminish, and the price will increase.

With my communities within my business sphere of influence, we are laying the groundwork to do this type of partnership or marketing. We've built the software platform with mPro. mPro is our effort to create a vehicle that crosses boundaries. For example, anyone on the mPro platform will have the ability to connect with anyone else on the platform.

We do this by creating business service referrals and a search function where you can search for people who offer services. We have big visions of what a platform should be and are launching a marketplace built into the platform, a marketplace where you can advertise your services, where you can say, "Hey, we do this. Do you have people you know who need this service?" You can refer to others and do interactive partnership marketing.

Proshark is my digital marketing agency, and our tagline is Intelligent Digital Solutions. We do everything in the marketing space, from software development to automation to digital marketing channels, social media management, website creation, website development, and customized web products.

Our SaaS platform, mPro, is a referral-based marketing, community-based marketing, and partnership-based marketing platform. On mPro, not only can you communicate with your customers, but you will also be able to reach out across businesses and entities to communicate with those businesses. These connections create a synergy that allows you to continually reach more people.

Additionally, we have the digital marketing side, which is all of our services. We're a full-stack agency, from software development and automation to web design and development. Proshark drives the development of mPro, but at some point, mPro will eclipse the marketing agency.

mPro is a marketing department replacement or augmentation that helps companies in an ever-changing digital world where you need expertise to reach your ideal consumers. mPro supplements what you need and where your company is lacking and provides the entire backend your company must have to operate efficiently and effectively.

And then, there's our roadmap. I have a larger roadmap, but our main roadmap goes to the development and the launch later this year. From the launch, we will move into the white label space to be able to offer other companies and agencies the ability to create a centric hub around what they're doing and the focus that drives their company. mPro is a new way to look at operating in today's complex and complicated business environment.

We have an ambitious roadmap for mPro that will benefit all business owners and marketers. Artificial intelligence is the ability to automate processes and services. We are building the ability to machine learn within the mPro platform. Our goal is to provide AI to almost every business out there because AI is currently not affordable for smaller businesses, marketing companies, and other agencies.

Automation will be key to efficiency and profit. Therefore, we'll offer an AI component where the machine itself learns the best channel for reaching customers and figures out the best channel for reaching out to other companies in a closed sphere or relational model. AI helps automate the process of reaching consumers in a way that's within the confines of big data privacy.

AI, in its current state, will only improve the ability to mimic and model data. This is where I started when I worked with Sony Pictures in their business intelligence group. Back before business intelligence was a popular phrase, we took all the data from Sony Music, Sony Pictures, and Sony Electronics and collected it all together. We were working to create a projection modeling engine.

Our projection modeling engine predicted that if I watched this movie and listened to this music, I would buy this type of electronic. Unfortunately, the project got scrapped before it got finished.

But that intelligent projection was something that small businesses still do not have access to because the data modeling and development effort around something like that is simply not affordable for them. Additionally, they would have to build a data structure, send out the mining and modeling tools, understand what those mining and modeling tools are, and figure out how to create the algorithms around those tools to come up with the right projections.

But imagine a world where I don't need cookie tracking because I already know that this type of person, who is in my database or in a database near me, has a proclivity for this type of activity. I know they will be inclined to buy this type of service or this level of service or this product or this type of product or products in this price range.

Imagine having access to those tools that have, to this point, been prohibitive because of the development effort behind them. And that's our goal. We hope to bring this full circle back to our community and add a community where business owners can make intelligent decisions and have automated outreach. That makes sense from an ROI perspective versus the gamble of paying for an ad only to get a negative ROI on it with zero response.

That's what most people are doing in the Facebook marketing space right now. They're paying for ads, and the ads aren't producing anywhere near what they cost. Facebook can't charge less because they don't have retargeting available anymore on forty percent of the market. They're about to lose the other sixty percent, so our communities have become exponentially important.

As a relatively young company, we have many disparate communities with whom we're working to create a single community. By this, I mean a hub community that we're getting ready to introduce to the world. And this hub community is where we're going to start. It is the genesis of our work, pulling all these resources together. The power of community is pulling all of those communities into one place and using the strength of our connections on Facebook with our connections on Instagram with our connections on LinkedIn with our connections on Twitter, and so on. mPro is the genesis that ties all of these communities together.

About the Author

Joel Phillips is an accomplished entrepreneur who serves as CEO of Proshark and founder/director of Strategic Advisory Board. Through both roles, Joel welcomes opportunities to help others launch and develop their own businesses, drawing on experience with digital marketing, software/app development, data, analytics, and cyber security. He's known for building and inspiring teams using a competitive and cooperative foundation to foster new ideas and imaginative solutions.

Learn more about Joel Phillips at proshark.com.

Elements of Community

Michael Sipe

I always had a side hustle doing real estate and passive investing, which is great because you can generate income and not have to be too hands-on. Separate from that investing and real estate success, I kept a day job consulting for corporations and for the government on various projects. I leveraged some of my engineering and piloting background, and what I discovered was that you have to network and build a strong relationship with people to be successful. Whether it's working on a real estate transaction or working on getting a product out to the consumer, it requires a clear understanding of what the purpose and the goal are.

The more I got into consulting work, the more I realized I was doing a lot more coaching than consulting, so I became an executive coach. My firm, Sipe Coaching and Consulting, helps senior managers and executives reach a greater sense of professional and personal development and growth so they can create greater impact on their work, business, and community.

My one-on-one coaching is where we establish what kind of mindset you want to shift toward, and then we determine the best plan and methodology to get you to that higher-level operating mindset.

In addition to one-on-one coaching, I have programs that help people grow professionally and personally. The one that has a lot of impact on people is the CEO Mindset for Growth and Abundance program. It's an online program that helps you accelerate into a mindset for growth and abundance.

Another program is the Intuition Project for Men. Steve Jobs, the former Apple CEO, was very influential in the tech industry. When you think of tech, you think of people with an analytical or logical mindset. Steve Jobs, however, was known for saying that intuition is more powerful than intellect. For the CEO of a trillion-dollar company to say intuition is that important means there's an opportunity to tap into a sort of sixth sense.

Intuition Project for Men helps you discover how to develop your intuition, and it focuses on your ability to have the right awareness and the right sort of consciousness. It creates the opening to receive these hits, ideas, and instincts. It teaches you how to reach out and get ideas that are outside of the logical process.

The third program is the Better Resilience program. By resilience, I mean managing your core energy and your attitudes with a focus on the power of the 40,000 neurons surrounding your heart. Your heart has over 40,000 neurons, its own neural net, that provide a mini-brain of sorts. When your heart is in control, it sends coherent information to your brain, and then your brain and your heart get into coherence or in sync. Your body starts to naturally restore and heal and becomes refreshed.

The Better Resilience program helps you discover how to get into a stronger awareness of your nervous system and how to tune that and get it aligned so it's at peace and in harmony. When that happens, you have better resilience, and you're able to handle stress and adversity in a more holistic way. That creates greater personal awareness and greater consciousness. This helps you avoid stomach ulcers, cancer, and many other maladies. The Better Resilience program provides a methodology to help you create a healthier life.

Those are three of my programs, but I like to leverage the business-opportunity mindset from my consulting and layer that on top of the coaching side. When you have a business-opportunity mindset, you find ways to grow revenue, you create out-of-the-box solutions, you see opportunities in crisis, and you discover ways to grow your business. Being able to see opportunity creates a sense of possibility for growth and abundance.

Like many solopreneurs, I use email and LinkedIn to build community. I also have a membership site, and I use my *Energy of Business Moments* podcast to help grow community. Those are more of a passive approach in the sense that they are forms of one-way communication, but they create more than just a following of people: They're ways to create an exchange of information that creates connection and value. My communities are geared toward providing something useful for people—whether it's a thought for the day, a brilliant business expansion idea, or a stress-reduction program—it's something that they can take away with them and continue to use, and they provide a daily or monthly program that makes them feel connected to others.

We have a saying in my coaching community that every client is our teacher and student. We all go through this thing called life, and we handle our experiences differently. So, for a community, seeing how we each handle these experiences differently provides a way for people to have an expanded awareness through other people's views and perspectives. This creates a greater group consciousness. It's how I grow, and it's how others grow—by being exposed to how other people handle adversity, how they take advantage of opportunities, how they deal with stress, and how they deal with life issues that come out of the blue. In our membership forum and our community calls, we have the opportunity to share insights, perspectives, and lessons learned. We create camaraderie and a sense of belonging, and we connect to something bigger than ourselves.

Community starts with two people exchanging ideas, sharing thoughts, and having a conversation. When we are in business, it boils down to what somebody else needs and if we can provide value or have a positive impact on them.

Often, to build a community, you have to start with a two-way exchange of information—just a conversation. This could be talking to a postal clerk when you're shipping a package. It could be talking to your auto mechanic who's repairing your car, it could be talking to a friend at church, or it could be talking to a stranger on the street who happens to appreciate the beauty of that particular day. Community starts with just one other person. When we get in the habit of having open conversations with strangers, or people with whom we might not normally talk, we have each other's attention. That's when we start to build community.

We can then expand and scale that community. That expansion creates a community where you consider how you can provide not only for this one person but also for other people and how you can create a product or service that makes people feel like they're getting some value, that they're getting a product or a service that changes their lives for the better. The community is based on the idea, "If I give, I receive."

The act of giving is more powerful than receiving in terms of how it affects our bodies and our brains. Our thoughts and our feelings are amplified when we give to others. The community environment is built upon giving to each other, and it feeds and grows. It's an internal force that creates momentum: The more that's being given in a community, the stronger that community becomes.

Now, we all have our personal styles, and how I interact with my community might be different than others. I like to bring a little humor at the beginning and a little bit of get-to-know-you in a community like, "Hey, how was your day? Tell me about what your biggest challenge was today?" and just go around the room and see what other people are going through and celebrate some successes and commiserate over challenges. The main thing is to create an opening for that dialogue and then always acknowledge and validate (A&V) what somebody else is going through because that creates a bonding experience.

I like to make sure that in my community, we acknowledge and validate each other. It doesn't mean we have to agree with everything that somebody is saying, but we can appreciate where they are coming from and why they are saying what they are saying. By validating them, they feel deep down that somebody understands them to some degree, and that forms a strong bond. To have a community, you must have those strong bonds. Therefore, I like to create an atmosphere where we lighten it up with a little humor, talk about some of our issues, and then zero in on the attitudes and energy that people are expressing.

I'd like to talk a little bit about energy because there are so many different definitions of energy. When I talk about energy, I'm talking about our thoughts, our emotions, and our actions. So, for example, if somebody tells you that you did something wrong, your first thought might be that you messed up. Your emotion might be an embarrassment. And then the action that comes out of that might be blushing of the cheeks, meaning that the body was signaled electromagnetically to release certain chemicals within the body that caused our face to become flushed. If you think of the thought that you did something wrong, the embarrassment of doing something wrong, and then the corresponding action of the body—that's what I mean by our energy.

It can also be an action that we willingly do. For example, maybe we become upset when somebody points out something because we're embarrassed, and so we become defensive in our demeanor. That's an action we might take.

Another example of energy is on the positive side: Somebody compliments our work after we put a lot of time and effort into a particular project. Our thought might be, *Oh, I was recognized for doing good work*, and the corresponding emotion is one of joy, *Wow, I feel great!* And then the action might be to say, "Hey, thank you for saying that," or the action might be to take on an even bigger project now because you feel empowered because you were successful at this one project.

Understanding energy is the understanding of the thoughts, emotions, and actions we take. When we're building a community based on camaraderie and the exchange of ideas, we can raise the overall energy of the community by acknowledging and validating that people are going through some tough or challenging times or joyful and wonderful times. The more we acknowledge and validate that, the more we're raising the energy of the group, and that helps build and create that stronger bond I mentioned earlier.

In addition to that, I use my powerful listening skills to listen to what's behind the words when people are talking—the energy. And I use my intuition to identify why someone is saying what they are saying. When somebody says something, that first harmonic of the wave of energy that comes from the mouth of someone—the first wave in that harmonic signature—is the actual words that were said.

So, if you remember back to your teenage days, maybe you were sitting on the couch, and you had your feet up on the coffee table, and your mom came in and told you to get your feet off the coffee table. The words *get your feet off the coffee table* are the first harmonic. There's a meaning in those words. The second harmonic is the emotion behind those words. So, if our mom yells at us to get our feet off the coffee table, there's an emotion of anger or frustration in that. The words have their own meaning, but the emotion adds an additional layer of information that we can be listening to that tells us about the emotional power or the emotional energy behind what's being said.

When I'm listening to someone, the third harmonic that I like to listen for is why someone is saying what they're saying. So, if a boss has an employee come to tell them that a vendor was late with their product again, well, the vendor was late. Okay, that's factual. That's the first harmonic—words only. Then the second harmonic might be, *Oh, I detected a little frustration in my employee.* Now you can go down and explore the emotion behind why the employee is frustrated. The third harmonic is the most important part: Why are they saying that? In this particular instance, this employee has said that this vendor is now, for the 16th time, late in delivering products that the company needs to get their own products out the door. They've been running late for a long time, and something needs to be done about it.

It's very powerful when we listen to the thoughts and what the specific words convey in the first harmonic. With the second harmonic, we're listening to the emotion of why they're saying something. Sometimes there's not a lot of emotion, maybe it's just purely factual, but there are other times when there's some hidden emotion that we can sense with the inflection of the voice or with the raised eyebrows, but there's something that we can sense that's an emotion attached to the words. Then the third harmonic that can be there is why they're saying what they're saying. Why are they sharing what they're sharing?

I like to identify those feelings and actions of our energy. That's how we create space where people can identify that energy, and then they can actually relate to it in a community. When they hear other people talking, and they hear the why, that gives them something that they might reflect on and go, *Oh, I've had a similar experience. Oh, I'm not much different than they are. Hey, let me tell you how I handle that situation.* Therefore, listening is very powerful in a community.

I think the other thing that's interesting is that human emotions haven't changed over the span of the history of mankind. We still feel anger. We still feel joy at the birth of a new child. That's what makes our community so unique is that we strengthen bonds between people. We often share the same energy or see a form of energy that we want to bring into our experience more and more. In a community setting, if we're raising up our collective consciousness, then what we're doing is providing a real-life, tangible "I can see somebody else expressing qualities in their life that I would like to express in my life. How can I get more of that? How can I bring more of that into my life?"

If we see others as an example, we can replicate that ourselves, especially if we're listening and understanding why they're saying what they're saying. So that's a big part of why, in my community, we try to focus on listening to and understanding the energy behind what each person is saying. That creates the bond and the strength of a good community.

For a community, the first thing I would like people to learn about me, and the coaching methodologies that I use, is that it boils down to our personal energy—what kind of energy we bring to any situation throughout the day. Then the next level is one-on-one communication with somebody else. When we are communicating with somebody else, we are creating a two-person community, which can be very powerful.

A lot of my community work is spent creating one-on-one relationships with others. The benefit is that if they walk away from that communication enlightened or feeling better, then they are going to share that with those who they come in contact with later in the day.

It's a second-order effect, where I may not directly affect the person they come into contact with later in the day, but I will indirectly affect them because I have created a different consciousness for that particular person I was working one-on-one with. They then replicate that throughout the day in other venues and settings.

That's the primary, but then the secondary is the weekly community calls that we'll have. And that's where we get to have group discussions, dialogue, and bonding, which creates a stronger sense of community.

First, you're focusing on raising your energy to have that one-on-one conversation with somebody else, and the second is having a group community. I would say those are the two main venues where community is expressed in my work.

In the SAB wellness committee, what we're looking to do as a company, the Strategic Advisor Board, is to bring business owners and CEOs the opportunity to scale and grow their businesses with greater revenue. How we get there is a multi-pronged approach, which means taking practical, logical steps to grow the business.

When it comes to the leadership side of being a good manager, a good business owner, or a savvy investor, the decisions that we make need to use a holistic decision-making process. What I mean by a holistic decision-making process is we must have a holistic mindset. When we have a holistic mindset, we are using our logical, analytical left brain to deal with a business plan or execute a business strategy, and we're also using our right brain, which is the emotional side. The right brain considers things like: *Am I keeping my frustration or my disappointment in check? Am I emotionally aware enough to see that I actually have a lot to be grateful for today? Am I recognizing that we have some new business opportunities that we've grown in the last two months, so I'm going to have a sense of gratitude and appreciation?*

When we are operating from *What would it feel like if I had that business growth?* then we're coupling the logical left brain with the emotional right brain, and when we do that, we raise our overall energy—the emotions, thoughts, and actions. And when we are in a space where we feel elevated emotions, we are sending specific information to our brain, and that information creates openings. And that opening is hearing other ideas come to us, either locally or non-locally, in the form of intuition.

Intuition is a third aspect of holistic decision-making. There's the logical, there's the emotional, and then there's the intuition. When we have higher-level energy, we can tap into all three and make much better decisions. And when we make better decisions, we create a better mental state. And that better mental state creates a better state of wellness.

The Strategic Advisor Board realizes that we need to have a better mental state of wellness for our business owners and for our CEOs. We hear over and over again that business owners and CEOs feel alone at the top. They're the ones who are ultimately responsible for making the decisions for the business.

Sure, they can delegate a few things, but the overall success of the company rests on their shoulders. It's not to say that they're lonely. They may have plenty of contact with family, coworkers, and clients; however, what they don't always have is the ability to have someone who has their back and can appreciate the challenges that they have at the top. And when you don't have someone that you can share your experiences with, you often feel alone.

The SAB Wellness Community is designed to help address how one can feel mentally well in a top condition as a CEO and business owner. Basically, what we're doing is trying to help business owners and CEOs feel like they're going from good to great in their mental capacity and their mindset, which creates greater health and wellness for them.

When we say the SAB Wellness Community, we're talking about building a community of like-minded people who are committed to elevating their mindset so that they feel like they are part of something bigger. And while they may not be able to see it in front of them right now, they have 20 other people who are in their group who are going through the same thing. They are collectively solving problems together and elevating their mindsets.

The beneficial effect of elevating our mindset is multiple, but the one thing that really helps is that it translates into better health for us. I think a lot of people know that when we are angry, frustrated, and stressed out, the sympathetic nervous system of our body is in control and dominates how the body regulates itself. It's producing a lot of chemicals that are good for fight-or-flight environments, but we're not in fight-or-flight environments throughout the day. We're actually in pretty peaceful environments, but it's when we assess those environments as being stressful and challenging that we go into fight-or-flight mode, and our sympathetic nervous system is driving our body into that kind of condition. The chemicals produced from that, including cortisol and other similar chemicals, while good at the moment, are not good for the long term. They hurt our bodies, and we may develop ulcers, cancers, and other health challenges because of our mental state.

What we're trying to do in the wellness program is help people see that they can manage their energy, thoughts, emotions, and actions better. And when they do, not only are they making better decisions, but they're creating a subconscious response in their brain where the parasympathetic nervous system takes over and does its normal function of restoring and healing the body. Obviously, if we have a good night's sleep, it's very nourishing. But during the day, if we can have those moments where we are able to bring in some practices for managing stress, then we are healthier mentally and physically.

That's the goal of SAB Wellness Community—to create an environment where people can share and become a part of growing wellness for small businesses. What that does is help the individual, but it also helps the company at large. It's a key component of being a small business. How do we grow? Well, not only do we grow physically, but we also must grow mentally, and that's a focus of the SAB Wellness Community.

There is more information on our webpage. Near the bottom is a SAB Wellness Community link that takes you to the SAB Wellness Community page. There, you can sign up and become a part of the community. It's one of commitment and effort, and we have so many commitments throughout the day, but it's important to prioritize our health, our wellness, and our life. We ask that people come committed, willing to grow, and be a contributor and part of a wonderful, loving, caring, expanding community that will allow people to benefit and benefit mankind. We plan to roll that out in August of 2022.

As humans, it's easy to ask ourselves, *What's in it for me?* From a community perspective, it's important to have a culture of community within our business. I'm grateful that I get to hear so many stories of people getting past themselves, and they start seeing some of that negative energy that isn't theirs, but they have attached it to themselves and bonded with it. When they can get past that, it's so rewarding to see that happen. When a group of people can see that happen, now you're talking about a community with impact. It's not just about who somebody wants to be; it's who they are and how they can get to being somebody they want to be.

I enjoy being in a community because I get to see transformation professionally. I get to see so many people who are going from being good leaders to being great leaders because they have leveraged some of the values and the benefits of a community. When you create a community in one setting, you want to replicate it in other settings. A business that has its own community has its own sort of soul and its own vitality.

A community centered around one small business is very powerful. When adversity comes, you don't have just one person solving the problem: You have a team of people solving the problem because they all are invested in that community. When we build a culture of community within our business, we become an advanced business because we are able to adapt, we're able to persevere, and we're able to see new opportunities and expand because we're doing our work collectively rather than individually.

About the Author

Michael is a business and life coach with a passion to help create abundance in business and one's personal life so that one has greater purpose and work/life balance.

Michael has trained, coached, and mentored thousands of people for over three decades. Michael's strengths are in creating an expansion mindset, fostering a workforce that is engaged, enthusiastic, and profitable and using his keen intuitiveness to integrate business systems in a holistic manner that compliment a scaled capability for hyper growth.

Michael is the COO of The Strategic Advisor Board as well as CEO of other coaching and consulting brands under his company, Michael Sipe LLC. Michael is a 3x international bestselling author and 4x bestselling published author with his current book, *Out of Dad's Box: How to Break Free from Parental Control and Transform Your Life at Any Age.*

Learn more about Michael Sipe at sipecoaching.com.

Start Your Own Communities

MIKE STEWARD

My company is called Vision Fox Business Advisors and is designed to help small and midsize business owners meet their goals. The business has three main divisions.

The first division is the business brokerage where we help mid-size businesses go to market, put their marketing package together, find what a buyer profile looks like, and then begin marketing their business confidentially. We work with prospects who come in looking to buy a business similar to what we've described in a generic sense. We qualify the prospects and get them to sign nondisclosure agreements, working them through the process that we have to help them make a decision, go through due diligence, and eventually purchase the business that we have listed and transfer ownership.

The second division is business coaching. Through coaching, we help some of those same potential buyers, or in some cases sellers, understand how to grow their businesses and make their businesses more valuable. We also help them get away from the daily grind of being in the business like they had to be when they first started as founders. We help them graduate into more of a C-level type of position within their business.

And then the third division is helping franchise owners grow their franchises, sell their franchises, or compare franchises, looking at where their personality and skill sets may fit to plug into a franchise system as a means of being an entrepreneur. That's really kind of what it boils down to.

What sets me apart is my experience and perspective. I have started a few businesses from scratch on my own. I have also helped transition businesses from private or independent brands into franchise brands. I work with about thirty franchise owners as their business coach, and I think what sets me apart is my breadth of experience of being in their shoes but not being too close to the business.

I owned a business for several years with my ex-wife. As business partners, we lost focus on other things in our lives and got buried in the business. So, I've been in those shoes, and now I know how to get out of that situation and help others do the same.

I really help owners have a different perspective. That is probably what I'm best at—offering that different perspective to help them get their business sold or help them grow their business.

The role of community in business is twofold. One, helping business owners understand where they fit in the community. And by that, I mean that I've worked with several prospective buyers for businesses that had been listed, and the business just wasn't the right fit for them. From a community standpoint, I don't think that they could award (you may want to remove award and put "have worn" that badge of being the owner of that business within their community because it wasn't in line with who they were, or who they even wanted to evolve into.

The second role of community is the role it plays for me. I've always been involved in my local community. I'm the president of several boards and volunteer within business-specific industries that I've been in. Being involved in my community has helped me personally develop, and I have always received double whatever I give when I get involved in a community.

Recently, as we've all evolved into the digital world even more due to COVID, I am now finding the groups of people that I want to be involved with digitally, which I find just awesome. I have friends in Australia who I never would have met. We exchange ideas. We exchange personal stuff, and we now have access to a bigger community that we probably didn't have access to before COVID.

When it comes to specific digital communities, I am involved in LinkedIn and Facebook. Facebook is a completely different community where I engage with business owners on a more personal level. When I became a certified life coach (I'm also a certified business coach), my coach at the time chuckled and said that life and business are the same from a coaching standpoint because they all mesh together. Your personal problems come to work, and your work problems come to life.

I find that LinkedIn is quite a bit different than Facebook for building a community. Although we may talk a little bit differently on LinkedIn and showcase in different ways, those same people often share different aspects of their life on Facebook in a different manner. Those are my two biggest online communities. Locally, I'm involved with the Chamber of Commerce on kind of a big level and see how different businesses are performing based on our local economy.

Another thing that I don't always think about as a community, but it absolutely is, is my podcast. The main reason I started my podcast is that I get to speak to some really cool people.

For instance, if I list a business for sale, and let's say fifty prospects come looking at the business, there are some really cool people in that mix of fifty. Some disappear, and we don't engage at a deep level, but they are all fascinating: the experiences they've had, where they've lived, the goals that they haven't met, the goals that they *have* met, and where they came from.

And the same with business sellers. I get an intimate look at why they're selling their business, how they started their business, and behind-closed-doors types of insight into their life. Often that's transitioning into retirement or relocating or some other neat event that we all dream of hitting those milestones in different ways.

Additionally, the people who seek coaching are incredibly interesting people, and so is where they're trying to take their lives to. I found that I have a tremendous amount of intrigue and respect for the variety of businesspeople in my life. I wanted to be able to share those experiences, and that was the whole reason behind the podcast.

I essentially created the foundation out of a few canned questions, like how do you stay healthy? And I think secretly, when we see somebody who's grinding out a tough lifestyle of entrepreneurship, we all want to know what they're doing that we're not that maybe we can learn and grow from. Or what KPIs do they have in their business? And how did they go from zero to X in five years?

The premise is to engage and have a great conversation. I've had great conversations with people over the years by engaging with a variety of businesspeople, but to strategically have that with some very interesting folks creates three opportunities.

One opportunity is to motivate. Maybe there's an entrepreneur out there who just needs to hear that they're not alone. The second is to share ideas. There have been some incredible health and wellness ideas that have come out of my podcast. The third is letting other entrepreneurs and business owners see through the lens of another business owner and view how they're positioning their lifestyle for success.

My first word of advice for starting an online community would be to truly understand your purpose for starting an online community. You must know what you are trying to accomplish. I think getting clear on that is the first step because that drives all your other actions.

The second would be to move forward. That's often my advice with coaching clients or business sellers: If you understand the purpose, move forward today, and not a month from now. Today is the day to move forward, but only if you know the purpose of it.

Third would be to go wide. There are a lot of really cool people out there you can find if you're open minded. I'll go back to the example of my friend in Australia. He and I could easily have never met, but we did, and he introduced me to another person in Texas, and without him, she and I never would have met. So, go wide enough within whatever connects back to your purpose to make sure you're not excluding those who could add value.

The last thing that comes to mind is to be open to variety in your community. Maybe that's similar to going wide, but I've learned so much from people in different industries that I know makes me better both in business and personally. Be open minded and pay attention to make sure it aligns with your purpose, but it doesn't have to be super niched to have a community that aligns with whatever your focus is.

To get involved in a local community, I suggest you find something meaningful to you, and that could mean so many different things. Meaningful could mean rescuing animals. It could be a health concern or health related, or it could be something that directly relates to your business.

I've always been very involved in the national, state, and local associations of realtors. When I had a real estate company, I felt like that industry gave so much to my family and me that I wanted to give back.

I've always tried to live in such a way that whatever I take from, I give at least an equal amount back. My driver at that point was to make sure that I was contributing to something that contributes to me. That kept me driven to keep engaging.

I get way more out of being involved in that community in probably fifteen different aspects of my life than just that specific industry. Therefore, I think the most important thing you can do is find something meaningful to you for whatever reason it may be. It may be going in with non-selfish motives, but I can guarantee you will leave with more than you brought unintentionally.

It's important to understand, before you even get out of bed, what the purpose of your day is. That's kind of a big statement, but you must know at least your broad purpose for the day. What's your reason to wake up in the morning and put your feet on the ground? Almost everyone has to-do list of some sort, but make sure your day is meaningful.

I have an alarm that goes off on my phone every morning at 8:30, and it's a reminder to create meaning and value. It says, "Be Intentional. Live, Love, and Matter." I try to live every day with that mantra. That would probably be my best advice, whether it pertains to running a business or being part of a community or just engaging with your family.

My "why" is *freedom*. For me, that covers so many things. That means freedom from having to depend on healthcare when I'm seventy years old. That's the hope to have rules in my life that help me operate in a fashion that allows me not to be dependent on healthcare, whether it's medical needs or prescriptions. That means freedom from being able to make the right decisions of what type of work I want to do and to make sure that I'm able to do meaningful, enjoyable, fun work most of the time on my terms. I want the freedom to do that versus having to just get a job or take a job or take a new client.

It also means the freedom to make choices that align with what I expect out of each day and what I expect of my remaining years left on earth to play this wonderful game we get to play every day.

I have a fifteen-year-old son, and I'm showing him examples that supersede the examples I was shown and that's not always easy. I'm trying to upgrade his life to make sure he sees the best way, at least the best way I have the means to understand, of what life should look like.

About the Author

Mike Steward has been coaching business professionals in various roles since 2001. In addition to his own startups and acquisitions, he has helped many owners and sales professionals across industries grow their businesses. He has started and operated five new businesses from inception to exit. In addition, he has helped launch two major franchise brands while staying on as a COO, President, and Vice President during post-launch stages. During the past fourteen years, he has worked closely with close to one hundred business owners in the ever-changing industry of real estate.

Learn more about Mike Seward at mikesteward.com.

THE STRATEGIC ADVISOR BOARD

The Strategic Advisor Board is a dynamic team that partners with your business to create custom strategies to help you grow your business on multiple levels. We look at the core foundation and systems within your current business to refine approaches, establish cost-saving measures, and ensure your systems are functioning at the highest efficiency and profitability. We add value to your business to place your business in the best position to implement strategies to scale.

We help businesses emerge from the growth to scale. When a small business grows, resources are added, employees are hired to serve more clients, and strength is added to the business within operations. Scaling your business is where you reframe your brand, automate many of your practices, and create strategic partnerships to begin the process to expand your influence in the marketplace. A comprehensive strategy, a team to support your business, and a trusted network of business service providers is what the Strategic Advisor Board offers to help your business grow into an influential brand.

Our multifaceted and dynamic approach to partnering to develop custom strategies to grow and scale your business is unique in the marketplace.

Are you ready to take the next step in your business?

Learn more at strategicadvisorboard.com.